MW01479462

85
GRAMS

DARYL ASHBY

Tellwell Talent
www.tellwell.ca

ISBN
978-1-77370-351-0 (Hardcover)
978-1-77370-350-3 (Paperback)
978-1-77370-352-7 (eBook)

Dedicated to the memory of
Dale Stuart Elliott

CONTENTS

PROLOGUE

I'm out of control!

—Arthur James Williams

The evening of November 30, 1977, was not a busy time for the traffic controllers at the Vancouver International Airport. The high-level clouds from the early afternoon had changed to fog with light rain. According to meteorologist Tom Gigliotti, who was on duty with the Pacific Weather Centre at the Vancouver Airport that evening, one feature of concern was a low-pressure system west of the Haida Gwaii Islands, formerly known as the Queen Charlotte Islands. Local forecasts offered no encouragement for incoming or outgoing flights, as the same weather system was predicted to linger for several days.

Commercial traffic had slowed to a trickle, with everything on the tarmac either loading or unloading its manifest. Those with private aircraft had found the comforts of home far more attractive than the thrill of beating the odds.

Except for Arthur James Williams.

Settled in to his Cessna, Williams picked up the handset to his radio and contacted Norman Daynor, the traffic controller on duty.

Daynor thought it was strange that such a light aircraft would attempt to fly into the kind of weather that was bearing down on the area, but he had no knowledge of the pilot's experience, and it was not his place to question the wisdom of an individual. Later, he would recall that Williams took an exceptionally long period of time at the end of the runway before accelerating.

"Vancouver Ground, Golf, India, Whiskey, Quebec."

"IWQ, ground," Daynor responded.

"IWQ south terminal taxi clearance Nanaimo with Oscar," said Williams.

Once airborne, the plane moved over the wetlands to the west of the Vancouver airport and swung southwest towards home. Norman Daynor heard Williams contact the Control Center, to which Daynor responded, "Say your destination and altitude."

Williams replied, "IWQ, westbound to Nanaimo, leveling at 4,000 feet."

Daynor clarified Williams' current position and reminded Williams that his directional transponder had not been turned on. A few moments later, Daynor picked Williams up on his radar. "Okay, I see you there, about four miles west, heading towards Nanaimo, but I'm not getting your transponder."

Williams replied, "IWQ, yeah. I've run into this problem here before. I'll try it again a few miles out."

A minute or so later Daynor acknowledged receiving his transponder signal. At precisely 9:15 p.m. Daynor noted that Williams had commenced an unauthorized turn. He radioed Williams inquiring what his intentions were.

"I'm experiencing problems with my ADF (auto directional finder) and am returning to Vancouver."

"Yeah, okay fine," Daynor replied. "I kind of wondered where you were heading there."

Daynor asked Williams if he would like a vector (magnetic compass heading) to the airport, and Williams replied that he would just proceed back to the VOR; a lit marker on Westham Island. When he asked

Williams if he had the airport in sight, Williams replied that he did not. Next, he asked Williams his altitude. It was 2,500 feet.

Daynor gave him the current weather at the airport. "IWQ, Vancouver weather is measured, 1,000 feet broken, 2,400 overcast, visibility four miles, very light rain showers and fog."

By this time, Air Canada 217 was approaching Vancouver at seventeen miles out. Daynor began talking to a couple of other aircraft, as well as the tower, and during the process of the conversation, he looked back at the target on his monitor and saw that the Cessna had completed the right turn. He pointed out to the tower that it appeared that Williams was having some difficulty.

Daynor radioed Williams once again. "IWQ, are you between cloud layers?"

Williams' only response was "IWQ."

The tower came on at this point and confirmed that Williams was twelve miles southwest, and according to its observation, "He's got a problem and so do we."

Williams' right turn never straightened out and kept getting tighter and tighter until it became a stationary dot on the radar. Daynor radioed, "IWQ, how are you making out?'"

Twenty seconds passed until Williams' replied "WQ," recklessly dropping a letter from his identification. And then, with the last syllable trailing off, came these words: "I'm out of control!"

Daynor shot back, "Okay, just take your hands off the controls and let her relax a little bit there." Twenty-five seconds later, Daynor inquired, "IWQ, how do you read me?"

At this point, Williams' blip vanished from Daynor's screen.

Daynor immediately contacted the tower. "I think we just lost IWQ."

Not wishing to give up, Daynor tried Williams again. "IWQ, Vancouver. Do you read?" This he did twice, but with no reply.

Arthur James Williams had vanished.

CHAPTER 1:

TRUTH OR FICTION?

*When it comes to Art, I had no reason to doubt that he was telling
me the truth. However, if Art trusted you, he was always truthful.
If he didn't like the way you looked on a given day, he would just
string you a line.*

—Happy Laffin

Margaret watched as Arthur James Williams, her husband of twenty
years, crossed the threshold of their home one last time. He picked his
way across the fifty yards to the rental duplex they kept on their property,
a satchel in his left hand holding a few essentials and a couple of books
in his right that represented his latest source of study.

In the kitchen window of the rental Margaret could make out the
image of Shirley Ferguson gloating over her victory. Since she moved
in just shy of a year earlier, Shirley had been the primary source of
Margaret's real life drama; a secondary source was Art himself.

Known by those close to him, Art was a man with an oversized libido;
one that simply couldn't be satisfied by the average woman. Caring as
Margaret was, she clearly fell into that bracket. She had tried to reason

with him, but whichever brain he was working from at that moment seemed heavily clouded by his physical needs. Shirley on the other hand, had the stamina of a race horse plus an extremely liberal view of sex.

Fact is, Shirley's two boys were the product of her free and easy sex life with two separate men who desired nothing more than to relieve their pent-up emotions. Both gave no thought to the child they sired and certainly made no effort to represent the father figure either boy so dearly needed.

Just prior to her taking occupancy of the rental, Shirley had fled yet another relationship headed nowhere. Thinking each would be different from the other, she entered this relationship confident it would be longstanding. If only she knew Art's philosophy: 'To survive, one must be able to sever their ties with family and home without as much of a second thought or the courtesy of a farewell'.

Shirley gave no thought to the upheaval of Margaret's life; her own survival was paramount and she clung to the principle of being 'the fittest', by discarding relationships that stood in her way.

Margaret continued to embrace Shirley's boys as though they were her own. As Shirley, will attest, Margaret's inability to conceive was not her fault but a matter of Art shooting blanks, hence the boys filled a void in her maternal needs. Following school each day the youngsters would visit Margaret, chow down as many freshly baked cookies as she offered and then plunk away on her prized organ. Before they left, Margaret would review their day and coach them on homework, confident such moments would prove to be the only positive influence they'd have in their lives.

In time, Shirley became familiar with the man Art Williams, his abstinence from strong alcohol and non-prescription drugs were not an issue. It never bothered her that Art had been perfecting the design and distribution of the synthetic drug known as MDA for over twelve years under the very noses of the authorities. Fact is, Shirley relished living on the edge and participated in its production. The only occasion Shirley seemed shaken was the day Art vanished without as much as a peck on the cheek. This left her with two young children, an ex-spouse and a half dozen of the elite inner circle dangling precariously in a police web, each groping at straws for some semblance of direction.

Margaret and Shirley only knew a smattering of Arthur James Williams' formative years and like everyone invited into his confidence, neither were confident as to what represented truth or fiction.

Art Jr. was born December 31, 1924, in Failand, England but spent his early years in Somerset, southwest England. His father, Arthur Williams Sr. was an honest hardworking man, who expected a lot from everyone, especially his only male child. Despite professing a religious affiliation, Arthur Sr. practiced the biblical doctrine 'Spare the rod, spoil the child' to the extreme. Gladys, Arthur Jr.'s younger sister claims their father justified his lack of compassion as an aftermath of being gassed during the First World War.

Hardship was no stranger to the Williams family. Arthur Sr. worked for a time as a construction laborer, building a dam in Nailsea, north Somerset, but for the greater part of his life he made ends meet as a farmer. In 1927, the family immigrated to New Brunswick, Canada, where they set their hands to working a small farm. The children not much more than infants at the time were expected to keep the stables clean and help with household chores. The youngsters found life in New Brunswick appalling, so no tears were shed when seven years later the Williams family returned to Middlesex England, on the outskirts of London.

Not long after returning tragedy struck Art and his siblings. Sophia Cotter Williams, a kind and loving mother developed a non-malignant tumor that required attention but Arthur Sr., believing it would heal itself, stubbornly refused to take his wife to the hospital. By the time he relented and took her to the hospital, the tumor was bleeding so badly the doctor ushered Sophia in for immediate surgery. She died shortly after.

In 1936, Arthur Sr. was having trouble making ends meet, and with no one to care for his children while he worked, he sent them to live with his widowed mother in Somerset. They stayed until such an age as returning home became a viable option.

During the dirty thirties, British boys became men overnight by having to assume the role of a provider. As was the case with Art Jr., he left school in his early teens and signed on as an apprentice cabinet maker, remaining at home with his sisters Ruth eighteen months his senior, and Gladys, who was younger by two years.

There is little wonder Art became a man who challenged and was equally challenged by all forms of authority. To those he disliked, his words showed that truth and fiction held common weight. "I rebelled against the structure of a society that assembled armies and inspired wars," he would tell friends, "and, for being such a kid, I was placed in a reform school for delinquent boys. I was incarcerated in Horfield Gaol at the age of fourteen for breaching the rules of society." His sister Gladys offered clarity to his comments: "When Art was about fifteen he was working in a small town a short distance from where we lived. He didn't like the work so he quit and hitchhiked to Gloucester roughly 91 miles west of London. He was broke and hungry, so late one evening he forced open the rear door of the Greengrocers' and helped himself to a couple of cookies, following which he fell asleep at the back of the store. The owner arrived in the morning, found Art sleeping and turned him over to the cops. He was marched down to the county court, but because of his age and it being his first offence, he was assigned to a probation officer who escorted him home to his dad whose first remarks were: 'Give him to me and I will straighten him out.' The officer felt that leaving him in Dad's care would be a mistake, so he made him a ward of the courts, the latter of which placed him in a juvenile reform school."

He was released after a year and took up employment doing bench work as a joiner with the Bristol Ladder Co. He proved so talented with his hands that he was transferred from making ladders to fine woodworking for government contracts.

As mentioned, fiction played a significant role in Williams' life. He told anyone who would listen that he lied to gain entry to the British Army at the age of sixteen. His military records however record the truth: Arthur James Williams enlisted on June 3, 1943, at the age of eighteen.

Art's trouble separating truth from fiction may have followed him into the battlefields. In a letter he wrote he states he participated in a push behind enemy lines: "The attack was a diversionary measure, intended to offset enemy troops and the Siegfried guns. Throughout the night of Nov 21st, 1944, our battalion fought its way to the foot of an escarpment. As the morning of the 22nd dawned it was bitterly cold. Mixed snow and rain had been falling for hours and the entire area turned into a sea of mud. The only vehicles able to function were the weasels, (a low-lying track machine having a slot for the driver and a flat surface to support cargo) which carried out the wounded and ferried ammunition up to the front lines. Our Company was 'S' company and our objective was to secure the western tip of Hoven Woods while laying down fire to cover 'C' company as they fought their way into the village from the west. By 11 am the command of 'C' company had been decimated which ground the offensive to a halt. To get the operation moving forward, our commanding officer was ordered to cross two hundred yards of open mud and assume command of the floundering 'C' company. Consequently, the operation of 'S' company fell to me." While some of this account can be supported by photos of Art in control of a weasel, a large portion conflicts with his military records. In a separate letter, a year after he had been shipped to the killing fields of France, Williams wrote to his girlfriend Daisy Cook that he had been captured by the Germans but managed to escape and make his way back through enemy lines to Gibraltar where he boarded a troop ship and returned to England.

In another instance, he weaved a story to a friend where the Germans had captured him and were shipping him by train along with another fellow, each of them handcuffed to a separate guard. Eventually the guards fell asleep and between the two prisoners they managed to kill the Germans. Dragging the corpses behind them, they jumped from the train and hid in the brush beside the tracks until dark. With no implements to separate themselves from the guards, they dumped the Germans across the tracks and waited till a second train passed severing the guards' forearms at the wrists.

For the record, Williams' military records state that he was attached to the Duke of Cornwall's Light Infantry as a driver-mechanic and was "wounded in action August 4, 1944 by shrapnel" while serving in northwest Europe. He was evacuated three days later to the Halifax General Hospital in England, where he stayed until his release. Forty-seven days later, on November 11, 1944, he returned to his unit in Europe and on February 17, 1945 he was wounded again but this time by a bayonet to his left shoulder. He was not evacuated but treated in the field. According to Shirley Ferguson, Art clearly bore the entry and exit wounds of the bayonet.

It was suggested that Williams replaced the fear that consumed some men at war with a zest for confrontation; and that habit carried forward in his life until the day he vanished.

After the war, Williams continued to tell tales. He lied when he told friends that he had participated in the attack on Arnhem and then contracted as an extra in the movie *A Bridge Too Far*. He lied again when he stated he was one of the first to enter Auschwitz at the end of the war and as a result was called up to testify at the Nuremburg trials.

He told his friend and lawyer Don Bohun that he and George Orwell [the author of the book *Nineteen Eighty-four*] trained in the British Special Air Services [SAS] and were both sent on a mission behind enemy lines to commit acts of sabotage, robbery, and assassination. To expose the lie, Don asked Art how he addressed George, to which he replied 'George'. When Don informed Art that Orwell's real name was Eric Arthur Blair and that George was only his pen name, Art became furious that he had been tripped up. Art's military transcripts show no mention of the SAS.

The stories never seemed to end and were only fueled by his zeal to supersede an earlier tale. Happy Laffin recounted: "When it comes to Art, I had no reason to doubt that he was telling me the truth. If Art trusted you, he was always truthful. If he didn't like the way you looked on a given day, he would just string you a line."

One of Art's wartime buddies believed, "Art and I were awarded more because we survived than because of anything heroic. We both started in the Duke's Light Infantry and after most of our comrades were shot up, we were transferred to the next division. As before, that division was dispersed leaving only ourselves and about twenty other young fellows, so again we were transferred to the next division. This repeated itself about five times until the war came to a close, but by then there were only twelve of our original crew left.

"Williams had always taken credit for his survival because he stayed sober. A lot of the other guys would get drunk on whatever they could scavenge as they moved from town to town and invariably they would stick their heads out of the trench in a drunken stupor only to have a sniper put a hole in it. Williams and I made certain we kept our heads below the top of the trench."

Williams propagated the notion that he was one of the most underdecorated soldiers in the British Army, and if per chance his stories contained an element of truth, his military records would support such a claim and yet they don't. Records show he was honorably discharged May 31, 1951, after having been awarded the 1939/45 Star, the France and Germany Star, and the 1939/45 War Medal. They also show that twenty months before his official release, Williams' restless spirit led him back to Canada and west to Alberta where his life would take a dramatic turn.

Art Williams Sr. 1922
Credit: Gladys Little

Williams family departing for New Brunswick
Credit: Gladys Little

Art Jr. 13 yrs, sister Gladys 11 yrs.
Credit: Gladys Little

Art Sr. in New Brunswick
Credit: Gladys Little

Art Jr. Germany 1945
Credit: Gladys Little

Art Jr. Europe 1945
Credit: Gladys Little

Art Jr. Germany 1945
Credit: Gladys Little

Art Jr. on right
Credit: Gladys Little

CHAPTER 2:

HONEST WEAPON, COMMON MAN

He stole the lumber he used to build the barn out back of his property, but even so I don't think he would steal from the archery association.

—Ralph Harris

Art took work in a remote Alberta logging camp and before long Margaret Katherine McDonald, while serving tables in a local café, caught his eye. Standing 5'5", with chocolate brown eyes, striking black hair and her dark native complexion, Margaret was his senior by a year, but that made no difference to Williams: she was simply too much for him to ignore. The two were married on August 19, 1949, twenty-one months before his official release from the army.

Tragedy consumed their first year together when Margaret was diagnosed with tuberculosis. The disease left her one lung and three ribs short following three and a half years of hospital confinement. Suppressing his restless nature, Williams stayed close to home and took a job as a driver for the Jasper Dairies.

The day following Margaret's release, she and Art moved in with his sister Ruth and husband Victor Dashwood. Williams chafed at this living arrangement. It was no surprise when he and Margaret moved to the village of Ladysmith on the east coast of Vancouver Island before the year was out. Attached to her brother, Ruth and Victor packed up and followed a short time later, purchasing a home within spitting distance.

The Williams' first home was a modest 12- by 20-foot shack tucked into an alley behind First Street in Ladysmith's town center. According to Laffin, the shack's early days had been spent as a caboose following a fleet of CP Rail coal cars.

This was replaced on March 25, 1966 by a five-acre parcel on Westdowne Road which ran parallel to the Trans-Canada Highway roughly three miles south of Ladysmith. It was close enough to town to secure needed provisions, yet distant enough to enjoy a degree of seclusion and avoid the unwanted attention that comes with a small community. They took up residence in half of the one-level duplex while Art converted the other half into a rental suite.

As the war years faded against the bright glow of prosperity, there was no lack of work to be had. Williams found employment as a carpenter in the construction of the Elk Falls pulp mill, located a few miles north of the sports fishing capital of Campbell River on Vancouver Island. He took lodging in Campbell River through the week then made his way home on the weekends to be with Margaret.

Somewhat lonely, Margaret found solace gathering old bottles, jars, vintage glassware, coins and other collectables that she would resell to summer tourists in the one room cabin set just off the road on their property. Off-season she would venture away for a day or two with her sister-in-law Ruth, in search of new items to add to her collection.

Not long after their move to Ladysmith Williams had formulated an idea for an archery business. Archery had again become a fashionable sport. Hunting with bows and arrows had gained recognition as a limited-harvest method for game management in many Canadian and American jurisdictions.

Art and Margaret were exposed to the sport while residing in Edmonton, and discovered they had a talent for sending the arrow in the right direction.

Having witnessed so much carnage during the war, Williams had developed the fear of a nuclear holocaust. Believing if humanity were going to survive future wars, they would have to be fought in a primitive manner. In his mind, the bow was the only "honest weapon of the common man."

On May 25, 1960, Art registered 'Williams Archery Limited' with the B.C. Register of Companies. Incorporation papers listed himself and Margaret as directors in addition to Grace Bettie and Stephen Oliver Franks, both of Ladysmith. Williams' lawyer at the time, Edmond F.N. Robinson of Ladysmith, B.C., was a minor shareholder.

While this represented Art's first step towards financial independence, it also became the catalyst that exposed his anti-establishment behavior to the authorities. With this, his behavior would elevate him to the top of the RCMP's watch list.

For all his faults, Art Williams was a perfectionist. If he put his mind to doing something, he wouldn't quit until it was as good as it could get. Williams applied himself to the design and manufacture of a long bow that many considered superior to others on the market. His craft started in a shed located behind their home. He constructed a workbench and purchased a hydraulic press on which the first of his creations came to life. He purchased varied thicknesses of fiberglass cloth from DuPont to test the pull strength for a number of bows. His friend, Laffin mentioned, "I worked with him when he was developing the bow. Many of the first models would self-destruct on the initial pull." Art experimented with all sorts of glues and once hardened he would do his best to pull the laminated pieces apart just to see how well they worked.

Believing he could invent a better mousetrap, Art came up with his own formula for resin and with persistence he managed to blend just the right mixture of fabric and resin. Art evolved into a crazed scientist as he pored through his library of textbooks looking for the ultimate solution. He would drive ninety miles to the City of Victoria where he combed the public library and the University of Victoria library until he found what he was looking for. He discovered that a certain hardener not only cured the resin but also acted as a modifier and induced flexibility making it possible to get a relatively stiff laminate by using a small amount or, if desired, a laminate with greater flexibility by adding just a wee bit more.

"Art," Laffin says, "started to put out some mighty fine-looking bows that would stand up well to normal abuse." And when the orders for the Williams bow started coming in, Williams found that he could no longer maintain production within the confined quarters of his shed.

To allow for expansion, Williams applied for and received a $23,000 loan from the Industrial Development Bank of Canada. With it he constructed an eighty- by twenty-foot concrete block building at the front of his property, which was divided between an office, a clean room where he could do his lamination, and a general workshop. Some of the crude equipment he had been using needed to be replaced so he used some of the borrowed money to purchase two hydraulic presses and a couple of wood lathes. A bucket of resin can give off toxic fumes which will pickle a man's brains in no time so he installed an air exchanger in the laminating room that could move 7,500 cubic feet of air a minute.

Happy Laffin was called on to lend a hand with the grunt work and between the two of them they pushed out four bows a day. Before long the Williams Bow was regarded as one of the world's best. As his reputation grew, so did the demand for his craftsmanship. The popularity of the Williams' bow left them struggling to keep up with the orders. With a bright future in sight, Williams left the secure job he had at the Elk Falls mill to devote himself to the bow's production.

Williams concentrated on a design known as a re-curve and would doodle away for hours on full-sized renderings. He was determined to get it just right. Each limb of the bow had to be the same, not only in length, but also in its pull strength. He built a test range at the back of his home and kept tweaking the product until he had the law of physics worked out.

One of the first lessons that came out of those early sleepless nights was the need to maintain uniform tension on the bow throughout the manufacturing process, right up until the final cure of the cloth and resin mixture. He had a decent press but realized that too much pressure was just as damaging as too little. Williams envisioned a means of maintaining constant pressure across the head of the press. With a limited budget, he scrounged whatever he could, wherever he could, to keep his costs to a minimum. The idea he concocted was to affix a piece of three-inch fire hose to the upper head of the press, seal off one end and fit an air valve to the other. He then added 100 pounds of air pressure to the hose, which exerted just the right inertia to hold his lamination in place until it hardened.

Williams came up with a half dozen models, each with pull strengths ranging from thirty-five to eighty pounds. To be competitive, he sold his entry-level model for a paltry $35 plus change, with the top model approximately $85, FOB his Ladysmith shop.

Happy Laffin took a keen interest in Williams' success, but during the day he supported his family as a longshoreman at the Crofton sawmill. There he noticed how the freighters cast off their dunnage, used to cradle their loads. He started collecting the scraps of wood at the end of his shift and would take them over to Art's. Williams knew all the woods by name and started laminating a mixture into his bows. For the bow's limbs, Williams preferred the hard rock maple with its rich color and he favored old growth material with a fine grain. He dug deep into the pile until he found pieces that were free of cross grain.

Margaret wove most the bowstrings out of a Ban-lon material. Artistic by nature, she hand-labeled each bow with the Williams' logo plus details of the bow's length and pull strength.

But Williams wasn't happy just to manufacture a good bow, he wanted to produce the very best, and to achieve that he knew his bow had to out-distance his strongest competitor, Bear Archery, of Greyling, Michigan.

He immersed himself in the study of current and historical designs and materials, reading of the Turkish sultan Selim, who in 1798 set a flight record of 972 yards, 2 ¾ inches that had not been broken by 1960. Williams refused to accept the possibility that a bow made of horn and sinew, held together with animal glue, could be superior to the modern composite bows made with materials, adhesives and techniques unheard of in the eighteenth century. Williams held the opinion that the secret of the sultan's record lay in the arrow and the skill of the individual archer.

To aid in his quest, he contacted Jim Dewar of Nanaimo, B.C., who held the Canadian Flight Champion title at that time with a flight of 552 yards, 2 feet, 8 inches. Together they hoped to challenge the record by 1964. Laffin suggested the first thing Art did was to analysis the design of the sultan's arrows, then use their characteristics, but with a better spine to weight ratio.

When Williams was convinced that he had the right combination, he started travelling throughout the Pacific Northwest to compete with bows and arrows of his own creation. He was pulling a short bow with 150 pounds of pressure, but it was so powerful that conventional arrows as well as his own would flex and deflect off their trajectory. He would lose over half of his arrows with each competition.

Nothing seemed easy for Williams, but that never stopped him. He returned home to redesign his arrow focusing on one that was not too heavy but rigid enough to take the stress.

He heard that MacMillan Bloedel logging company had a shed full of fine grained spruce at its Powell River plant purported to be 800 to 900 years old. Laffin tells the story, "We were told it was left over from material cut for Howard Hughes' flying boat, the *Spruce Goose*. We got our hands on a few blocks, then Williams machined up a cylinder press that would punch out hollow barrel halves, which we then glued together.

There is no denying Art Williams was a brilliant guy. Nothing ever got in his way if he was determined to make something happen." If only he had created something fundamentally accepted by the masses, God only knows how he would have succeeded and prospered. For certain, history books would have written him up as the intelligent wizard that he was rather than the despised drug czar that he became.

His new arrows turned out to be lighter than the conventional ones, a little fatter up front than in the rear, but he could shoot them 600 to 700 yards with no deflection." Williams drove south of the border to compete in Portland, Oregon, with his new set-up, but unlike the prior events, this time he shook the very foundation of his competitors and got immediate recognition.

Both Margaret and he started breaking established records using equipment of their own creation. With success at provincial and national events, the popularity of the Williams bow reached new heights. The demand for Williams' arrows soon equaled that of his bows leading to the old-growth material from MacMillan Bloedel being consumed. Williams put out feelers for similar material and got wind of a half dozen old-growth yellow cedar logs that had been cut during the First World War but were still laying in the Caycuse Logging Camp near Cowichan Lake. Cedar had little to no market during the early 1900s; hence they served as a cushion onto which trucks could dump their loads of saw logs. Williams and Laffin found the massive timbers without much difficulty even though they lay buried by five decades of moss. They peeled back the moss in sheets then cut them into lengths before hauling them back to Art's shop where they morphed into new arrows.

In 1963, Art's notoriety made him an obvious choice to become the newly elected president of the Canadian Archery Association. Without wasting time, he resurrected the organization's monthly magazine and assumed the role of its editor-in-chief, with his long-time friend John MacNaughton, then owner of the *Ladysmith-Chemainus Chronicle*. Before the ink had dried on several of his publications, rumors surfaced that if Williams had his hand in the association, trouble would follow.

On April 17, 1967, the executive of the Canadian Archery Association, along with one representative from each of the provincial associations, met with four members of the board of the advisory council for the Federal Fitness and Amateur Sports Directorate.

The advisory council were the people who administered federal funding to national sports franchises and they took their day-to-day direction from the same government that would become a proverbial thorn in Art Williams' side.

In early April, the advisory council had been given notice that all financial support for national events sponsored by the Canadian Archery Association would cease until a meeting had been held by all executive members of the Canadian Archery Association, less one Arthur Williams.

The focus of the meeting was to discuss a report from the federal auditor assigned to monitor the association stating he had been unable to account for funds given to the association. With no solid evidence, the council was convinced that Williams had misappropriated the funds. The council made it quite clear that if the Canadian Archery Association wished to receive further funding, it would have to remove Williams as its president. Following an eighteen to one vote, the late Don M. Lovo, then vice president of the association, delivered the message to Art that his services would no longer be required.

Williams was not without supporters at the local level, but combined with a few loyalists in Quebec, no amount of debate could sway the executive's decision. Financial support from the feds outweighed any attachment to Arthur Williams as their president. A few executives saw Williams as a man who acted out his own personal agenda and this opportunity parlayed well as a way for them to even the score.

Those who knew Williams believed he could have been a modern-day Robin Hood. His nephew Allen Dashwood remembers clearly when his uncle was delivering milk in Edmonton: "He would give butter and milk to those who appeared to be in need and never ask for payment. He would just make restitution to the company out of his pocket at the end of the day." According to others who knew him, he would not hesitate to take from a government that so foolishly squandered tax dollars, but, equally so, he was not the type of man to steal from his peers. "Not entirely true," says Williams' close friend and fellow archer Ralph Harris. "He stole the lumber he used to build the barn out back of his property, but I don't think he would steal from the archery association."

Outright thief or Robin Hood, the badly shaken Williams moved on and turned his full attention to his thriving business, but within a short time that too came under attack.

DuPont had been supplying Williams' with fiberglass cloth and resin since day one, but there were rumors that, with the Williams bow making such a dent in the market, one of his largest competitors purchased the sole rights to the DuPont line of cloth and resin and then for obvious reasons refused to sell Williams what he needed. Within a matter of days, Williams' production ground to a halt.

Refusing to give up he borrowed more money, this time from the B.C. government's small business and loans program, following which he took the ferry over to the mainland and paid the science lab of the University of British Columbia a visit. He explained his dilemma to the professors and convinced them to enter a partnership to develop a new cloth that would rival that of DuPont. He then met with officials of Shell Oil, who agreed to work with him to develop a resin equal to that which he had been purchasing.

For much of society, if problems crop up, they seem to come in threes, but in Williams' case they proliferated like rabbits. Without explanation, the B.C. government pulled their funding only weeks after assuring him he had their support. This left Williams high and dry, with money committed to the university and no way of paying it. Before many days had passed, Art received a second letter advising him that the Industrial Development Bank of Canada was taking steps to call his loan and foreclose on his business. The dark underbelly of modern banking had been fully exposed.

Everyone who spent time with Williams knew that he had a short fuse, but this situation pushed him over the edge.

Margaret Williams
Credit: Gladys Little

Williams home on Westdown
Credit: Vancouver Appeals Court

Margaret's sales cabin
Credit: Daryl Ashby

Aerial of Westdown property
Credit: Vancouver Appeals Court

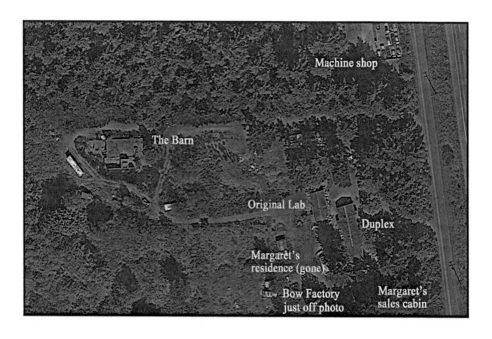

Art proudly displaying one of his bows
Credit: Daniel Ferguson

Williams Bow
Credit: Bill Sampson
Westcoast Archery

Art demonstrating a bow
Credit: Daniel Ferguson

Art testing bow
lamination
Credit: Daniel Ferguson

Art's bow factory
Credit: Daryl Ashby

CHAPTER 3:

DECLARATION OF WAR

Your Honor, I see that you are seated; therefore, I choose also to sit.

—Art Williams

Arthur James Williams had a disdain for authority of any kind, whether it be the overzealous preacher on a street corner telling him how to live his life or the puffed-up individual with a badge and a gun. He had a similar contempt for the federal government when they tried reaching into his pockets to seize a portion of his hard-earned money in the form of taxes. Art held to the belief that personal income tax was created as part of the 1917 War Measures Act and he quotes it was "... implemented only as a temporary measure to offset the enormous debt brought on by the First World War".

Since the day Arthur James Williams set foot on Canadian soil he had never filed the mandatory federal income tax form, and he certainly wasn't going to begin now. He felt so strongly about the issue that he published a paper entitled, "Declaration of Economic Warfare on the Government of Canada," a copy of which he fired off to Prime Minister Pierre Trudeau.

Although he refused to pay the government sales tax as well, to retain ownership of his property, he conceded to paying property tax. On more than one occasion he made the full payment in the form of coins. He'd show up at the municipal tax office on the last day that the taxes were due and ten minutes before the office closed. If they didn't take the coins, in his mind they had refused his payment. Needless to say, this made the clerks livid.

When federal tax enforcers had to descend on Williams' property to collect outstanding taxes, the local RCMP were called in as an escort. On one visit the collectors turned to Williams and asked to look at his books. He replied, "Feel free, there they are," pointing to a pile of ash on the ground. For all the feds knew, he had maintained a set of books but had burned them in protest. In Williams' mind, the pile of ashes said it all. He was not going to be paying income tax.

Williams' contempt for the law only fueled his enthusiasm to do battle. Taunt the taxman however, and most people can predict the winner. Revenue Canada has always maintained the freedom to rewrite the law as it sees fit. On this matter, Arthur James Williams was a slow learner as he believed he was wiser in the ways of the law than those who were paid to write it, so he continued to ignore the tax service's demands for a declaration of his income.

In 1969, Revenue Canada concluded Williams owed $57,000 in unpaid taxes, interest included. Attempting to outwit the feds, Williams declared personal bankruptcy, but by the time his notice of bankruptcy had been filed in court, Revenue Canada had already changed the locks on his archery factory, seizing both the structure and what they assumed were its contents.

To insure Revenue Canada gained nothing more than a shell of a building, Williams and his friend Happy Laffin had worked through the night preceding their visit to remove everything of value. They hid all the presses and lathes, even the electrical panel, in the woods out back of his property.

When the bailiffs found the building empty, they declared Arthur Williams the primary suspect, laying charges based on a single strand of electrical wire that they found on the property, claiming it was a remnant from the electrical panel.

Accepting the likelihood that the inside of a courtroom was going to become familiar territory, Williams set out to find a man who held a law degree but was not a slave to conventional practice. He found such a person in Donald Joseph A. Bohun.

Wearing his hair well below his shoulders, Bohun had the quiet, reflective demeanor of a man who had been taught to listen rather than be heard. His uniform was not the usual three-piece suit tailored by the society of court officials he had been groomed to navigate. Like most people associated with Art Williams, Don Bohun never exuded a look of power with expensive clothes, gold jewelry and European luxury cars. If you met him on the street, he appeared to be an ordinary fellow rooted in the anti-establishment ethos of the 1960s.

Members of the judicial system saw Bohun as a disrespectful bottom feeder. He rode to the courthouse on his motorcycle with his mandatory court attire rolled up in a satchel on the back. His clothes were well worn and looked like hand-me-downs to begin with, but by the time he unrolled them, they were anything but presentable. When his colleagues walked into the courtroom meticulously dressed, having carried their pressed robes in suit bags, Bohun would saunter in looking more like a street urchin in drag. He just didn't consider all the pomp and formality a principle function of law.

Following a brief introduction, Williams discovered that he and Bohun had similar backgrounds. Where Bohun had served in the Canadian armed forces as a paratrooper prior to seeking a law degree, Williams had his military experience in the British Army before settling in Canada. They held comparable views on government and the ways and means by which every individual had the right to interpret the law for his or her own self-preservation. Like Williams, Bohun felt the word "evil" was best left to the preachers. Those milling about the underworld had a different understanding of its meaning than the suit-and-tie fraternity who picked up their pencils at nine and put them down at five. Williams needed a man who was not afraid to take risks, and Don Bohun was not shy when it came to pushing the envelope. He'd spent most of his time in court defending those who were caught up in the drug trade so he was never viewed as a mainstream lawyer.

One account has Bohun defending a young fellow who'd been caught with a small amount of hash, and when given an opportunity to examine the evidence during court, Don popped the sample into his mouth and swallowed it without batting an eye. Because the entire case hinged on a small amount of contraband, the prosecution had no choice but to withdraw their charges. Bohun offers his first-person clarity:

"When giving evidence, the cop pulled out a hash pipe with a ball of hash delicately balancing on it. The ball was about the size of your baby fingernail, but from personal experience I knew it could not have survived the transportation and storage in the condition that it was presented. The accused then whispered to me that he didn't have any hash on him and that the pipe was brand new and unused when the cop had seized it from him. The prosecutor then passed the pipe and contents to me for examination, as was the practice in those days. I took the pipe in my left hand and to keep the alleged hash from falling, I took the ball in my right hand. I had suspicions that it was not really hash. So, I took a bite and I must say the cops had very nice tasting hash. The prosecutor and cop stood there stunned as I swallowed the whole thing but they said nothing at the time."

Bohun defended Williams on the charge of theft of federal property as it pertained to the machinery missing from his factory. According to Stanley Cross, one of Williams' close associates and a man currently hiding within the Witness Protection Program: "On the day of the proceedings, Williams drove to the Ladysmith courthouse with an entourage of hippies in tow. He was wearing an orange hard hat, and as he walked into the courtroom he grabbed the lone chair at the back of the room and sat down. As the judge entered the courtroom, everyone was asked to rise, but Art stayed seated. The bailiff demanded that he stand to which Art approached the bench and asked if the judge believed that all men were equal, the judge responded he did. Art stated, "Your Honor, I see that you are seated, therefore I choose also to sit." The judge then asked Art to remove his hat. Art replied, "Nope, it's part of my regalia, so, much like yourself, I would prefer to keep it on." By that time, the courtroom was in an uproar."

Bohun argued successfully that the prosecution had nothing more than circumstantial evidence upon which to base its claim. At the end of the day the judge dismissed the case on the grounds of "insufficient evidence to convict."

Even in victory, the experience had a profound impact on Williams, both financially and emotionally. For reasons never explained, he felt that Margaret had played some role in his downfall and immediately turned his back on her. In their circle of acquaintances, it had been no secret that their relationship had taken a turn for the worse. Life with Art Williams dictated that Margaret had to concede to his opinion on every issue, but they never fought. Yet, as Gladys Little, Williams' sister recalls, "Margaret was visibly upset when Art left her."

As mentioned, on May 4, 1970, Art walked into the bedroom he shared with Margaret, cleaned out his sock drawer and strolled over to the rental duplex, where Shirley Ferguson had set up house with her two sons. To add a second layer of separation to his relationship with Margaret, Art built a second cabin behind the duplex in which Margaret would reside. On July 20, 1971, Arthur and Margaret drove to the local courthouse and made their separation legal.

Although estranged, Williams maintained a watchful eye on Margaret. He transferred the ownership of their Westdowne Road property solely into her name and paid her rent for his use of the duplex so she had a source of income.

Shirley Ferguson was twenty-eight years old when she welcomed Art Williams into her life. She had moved to British Columbia four years earlier, having left her family's home in Saskatchewan to flee a bad relationship. After settling in Crofton, a small community south of Ladysmith, she took work as a waitress in a small cafeteria to make ends meet. She was a slim, attractive brunette, seventeen years his junior, and her two young boys, Terry James, born February 8, 1965, and Daniel Shawn, June 3, 1969, came as part of the package. Their mutual friend Gordon Loomis introduced her to Williams, and from that day forward Williams assumed the role of the boys' father.

With his archery business defunct, Art Williams became obsessed with the science of growing a perfect mushroom indoors and soon became recognized as an expert in the subject. His focus was on developing a hybrid oyster mushroom, a valuable source of nutrients that anyone could grow since it thrived on darkness and physical waste, commodities that were widely available. Williams mentioned to an acquaintance that he had perfected a way to grow the mushroom spores on saturated newspaper tightly rolled into a cylinder, again a material discarded in quantity by the average household.

Williams applied for a $70,000 federal grant from the same government who foreclosed on his archery business and he received it no questions asked. To him it confirmed just how arbitrary the feds were. On one hand, they put him out of business claiming he owed $57,000 in back taxes, but then they turned around and forked out $70,000 in public funds as if they were ignorant of the prior event.

To rub their noses deeper in the mire of their own incompetence, on June 12, 1972 Williams registered his new business with the provincial

Register of Companies as a society. By doing so, his British Columbia Institute of Mycology would enjoy a few tax breaks and numerous venues through which he could shelter money under the pretense of research and development.

The headquarters for the Institute was the same squatty unpretentious shed that first housed his archery business during its infancy, making it invisible from the road. The stated objective of the society was "to engage in mycology research and without limiting the generality of the foregoing, to study mushrooms."

Persons registered as directors of the institute were Gordon Loomis, a gentle, soft-spoken man who worked as a professor of mathematics in Nanaimo, Myron Zarry, a graduate mycologist then living in Ladysmith, Janice Hanman, a writer from Duncan, Ruth Loomis (Shorter), an editor from Nanaimo, Louis L. Brown, a carpenter from Nanaimo, Kristine Loomis, registered as a student from Nanaimo, Arthur Williams, and Shirley Ferguson. While most of the directors immersed themselves in his less publicized on-goings, a couple were caught unaware of his true intentions.

Don Bohun with his father
Credit: Don Bohun

Don Bohun 2009
Credit: Daryl Ashby

Shirley Ferguson
Credit: Shirley Ferguson

Daniel Ferguson
Credit: Daniel Ferguson

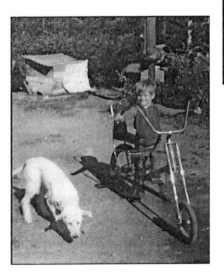

Terry Ferguson
Credit: Daniel Ferguson

CHAPTER 4:

HELTER SKELTER

I had a funny feeling about the whole thing from the start and had only let my name stand as a director because Gordon talked me into it.

—Ruth Loomis

During the weeks that followed the trial, Williams' redirected his energies from the world class archery business to taking full advantage of a demographic time bomb that was ready to explode.

The rear of his property had become a commune for a growing number of hippies, each looking for a way to fall off the grid and become one less cog in society's wheel. They found shelter in everything from dilapidated school buses, to tin utility sheds and canvas tents. While their vision statement was to live independent of the establishment and their social vices, they never hesitated to take handouts from Art and Shirley and seldom offered gratitude in the form of helping around the acreage. Art was adamant that each resident would give back something to the better good of their neighbor, so those that demonstrated a bent for freeloading were quickly shown the road with no invitation to return.

While not all the hippies displayed an insatiable thirst for a chemical high, enough did that Art became fascinated with the possibility of satisfying their cravings as a sideline to his mycology research. Many of the chemicals he needed for his legit research could easily be redirected for less acceptable reasons. There were no lack of volunteers within the commune willing to ingest his creations and fortunately for Art none of his potions brought on an early demise.

To assist him in his quest for a better mushroom, Art chose Myron Zarry a graduate of the University of Victoria with a major in mycology and a son of one of the hippies' resident on his land. In his mid-twenties, Myron was short and slight at five feet seven inches and 140 pounds, sporting a goatee with a thick mat of curly brown hair. Gordon Loomis on the other hand was Myron's senior by several years with a degree in psychology and electrical engineering. He was highly intelligent and held the dream of establishing a "free school" for those who were less fortunate and relished the benefit of a higher education. As a prerequisite to enrolling a child in his school, the parent would first have to attend an orientation meeting where Gordon shared his personal philosophy on learning, coupled with some basic psychology. Art met Gordon at one of these sessions which he attended on behalf of his adopted sons and there he debated everything that Gordon had to say. "Talk to Art for ten minutes," Gordon would say, "and your brain would never be the same."

Gordon and his wife Ruth had a home on Pylades Island, approximately seven miles east of Ladysmith by water. Of the Island, Ruth said, "For my husband Gordon, and me, life on Vancouver Island or any larger community for that matter, was just too harsh — the sounds, voices, smells, and lifestyles — so in the early 50s we retreated to this small piece of paradise. There was a big house on the island, but we built a small cabin, which was much easier to heat and care for. When company came to visit, they would make themselves at home in the big house." Their island would become a welcome retreat for anyone wanting to flee the hectic pace of city life; for others, it was an escape from the demons that held their bodies captive.

Ruth Loomis mentioned, Art started visiting their place for no purpose other than to kibitz with Gordon, who enjoyed the mental stimulation.

"They were two of a kind in a lot of ways," she said. "Like Gordon, Art was very cerebral, and the two became the closest of friends. I always felt Gordon had moments when he was a little too naive for his own good. Knowing Art as well as I do, I can see how he could recognize that in Gordon and take unfair advantage of it. Gordon seemed to have a sincere interest in what Art was doing in the area of mycology.

I had a funny feeling about the whole thing from the start and had only let my name stand as a director because Gordon talked me into it. I held no desire to get involved in what Art was doing and I made a point of cautioning my daughter Kristine after she started working for Art to be careful and question everything he asked her to do if she chose to get involved with the business."

In short order, Williams recognized Kristine's thirst for knowledge as well as her self-discipline when it came to staying focused on a given topic. He had already proven his ability to read people and the fact that she would be pliable to his work ethics made her more desirable as a key player in the expansion of his institute. At Williams' request, she donned a white smock and started digesting every book in his personal library that dealt with mycology, from the unusual to the most mundane.

"Art was idealistic about wanting to create food for those who couldn't afford it, and I had idealistic views on how to grow symbiotic foods. Fact is," says Kristine, "I had heard from dad that Art was going to be working with mycology, and I approached him and suggested he was going to be needing help. I had been reading up on mycelium at the local library, so I felt confident I could be of value. Art agreed and wanted to know what I would need if I was to work for him. I told him all I wanted was $100 per month to live on and I wanted to travel."

Ruth Loomis remained concerned about Kristine's relationship with Williams. She had recently lost her youngest daughter to a motor vehicle accident and had no desire to add yet another scar to her already torn emotions. "Kristine was only seventeen years of age at the time, and although she was living with her boyfriend, Lou Brown, I was still her mother and I felt responsible to keep an eye on her. As it was, I was unemployed so I asked Art if there was any work I could do around his property. He knew I wasn't afraid of hard work and I was handy with my hands. Being able to do most anything, Art put me to work building a concrete wall at the back of his property. That kept me within easy reach of my daughter."

Kristine became the institute's principal scientist, and Williams paid her well for her efforts. The fact that Kristine had never attended a public school or an accredited university changed nothing. The home schooling her mother had provided during her youth served her well.

Williams took great pride in his collection of reference books and often stated that his library held books you wouldn't find in the public library or the best of universities. For those questions he could not answer, he would engage the help of various scholars overseas.

In 1973, Williams arranged for Kristine to travel with Lou Brown to the Karl Weiss Institute in Germany. Lou was to take a three-week course on how to maintain a Weiss electron microscope, while Kristine was to learn how to operate it. After hours Kristine engaged herself with some of the greatest minds in scientific research and discovery. Ruth wanted no part of Williams paying for her daughter's travel and accommodation. "I had no wish for Kristine to be indebted to the man in any way, so I footed the bill."

After Germany, Williams sent her to a Pennsylvania conference focusing on mycology. There, behind closed doors, she was told that the conventional means of propagating spores was with horse manure, even though the practice left the spores contaminated. She and the others attending the session were instructed not to mention this finding outside the forum for fear it would turn the industry upside down. The reliability of truth remained paramount in Kristine's life, so she snuck the paper out of the conference so that Art could stay one step ahead of the rumor mill.

On February 1, 1973, Williams arranged for Myron Zarry to rent the building immediately north of his residence on Westdowne Road from its owner, George W. Attrill, with the intention of setting up a machine shop. He knew there would be specialized pieces of equipment that he could not readily purchase, so he would use this facility to manufacture his own. So out from the woods came the lathe and milling machine he had stolen from Canada Revenue when his archery business collapsed and into the machine shop they went to breathe new life into another of Art Williams' endeavors.

Williams jumped headlong into his new project and purchased all the equipment he might need. Nothing was too good for his efforts. The Weiss electron microscope alone cost him $72,000. "It was the only thing strong enough to see organisms," said Kristine. While awaiting the arrival of his new acquisition, Williams set to work constructing an 8,000-square foot, three story building towards the rear of his Ladysmith property. It was purpose built as a laboratory and further removed from peering eyes than the shed he was using. Williams was the sole architect but he called on his trusted circle of allies to form the construction crew. The building didn't trigger any alarms bells with the authorities since construction permits were not required at that time for projects beyond the city limits.

Williams worked side by side with Happy Laffin, Stanley Cross and Dale Elliott. Cross and his family were longtime residents of Ladysmith. While one of his four brothers chose a career as a helicopter pilot for the RCMP, Stanley was drawn towards the dark side of society. Elliott was known to the authorities as a senior prospect for the '101 Knights' biker gang and therefore knew most of the associated drug traffickers on a first name basis. He too was a man who woke up each morning looking for a reason to harass the establishment. If Art was considered a man with an oversized libido, Dale was known for having more mounts than the Pony Express. They represented ideal working partners.

The four men worked on the lab's foundation to bring it up to the main level before any outsiders were allowed within spitting distance of the building. Once the concrete forms were in place, Williams employed

Mayco Concrete to deliver all the cement they needed, paying the drivers a little extra to leave their curiosity at home.

The lab structure itself continued to come together with a high degree of secrecy. When asked what the purpose was for the small room in the far corner of the basement, which appeared to have no entrance, Art would respond that it was for the storage of chemicals. When Cross asked Art when they were going to cut a doorway into that area, Williams hinted that he would do it later. His answers all seemed plausible. For those who felt they needed to know, Williams made it clear that the main floor of the new building would be the headquarters for the B.C. Institute of Mycology, the top level would house its lab, and a workshop would be set up on the lower level.

Cross recalls, "What I could see was that Art intended to channel all the contaminated air through a system of ductwork that would then be treated to a fine mist. I now know his intention was to reduce any telltale odors to the bare minimum."

As time passed, Williams exploited every conceivable advantage offered by the government he so despised. He mailed off a request for exemption from paying taxes based on a claim that he was farming. In no time, he was given the green light with few if any questions asked. He asked for exemption from the dreaded excise tax, claiming he was going to provide Canada with the benefits of his scientific research. Again, the exemption was granted. He took full advantage of it by also acquiring all the materials he needed to produce a socially unacceptable substance. Art suggested, if one was to suggest the Canadian government was dysfunctional, that individual would be paying it a compliment.

Laffin adds, "He told me up front what the purpose was for the labyrinth of hidden passageways, trap doors, false walls and even the underground tunnels that led off into the forest out back of the lab and that through it all he would make every effort to thumb his nose at authority. He never hid from me his true intent for the building."

Christine Loomis (right)
Credit: Ruth Loomis

Art's machine shop adjacent to his residence
Credit: Daryl Ashby

Art's first mycology lab
Credit: Daryl Ashby

Art's first mycology lab
Credit: Vancouver Appeals Court

RCMP evidence diagram of Art's first mycology lab
Credit: Vancouver Appeals Court

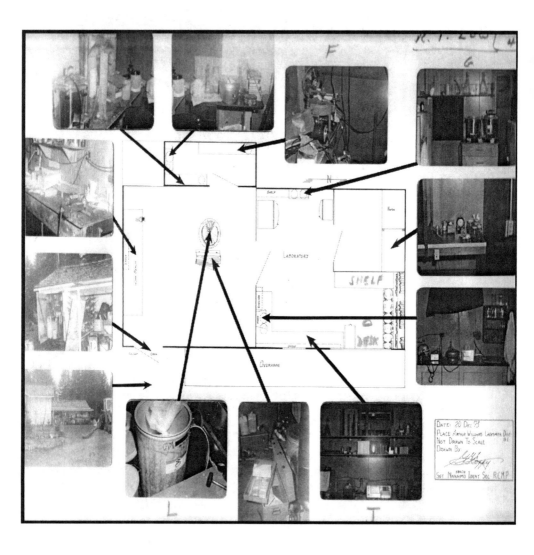

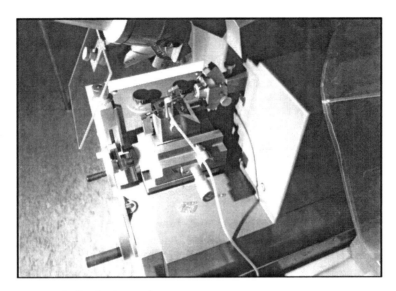

Art's electron microscope
Credit: Vancouver Appeals Court

Art's new barn / lab
Credit: Vancouver Appeals Court

CHAPTER 5:

THE LOVE DRUG

The MDA formula was originally a 1932 German recipe and Gordon Loomis copied it for Art from a book in the UBC library.

—Ralph Harris

By the mid-1960s, the Harvard psychology department was thrown into turmoil by Dr. Timothy Leary's research into mind-altering drugs that were beginning to flow, unregulated, through cracks in the U.S. law. One of the forerunners was a white, odorless, crystalline powder called LSD (lysergic acid diethylamide), more commonly known on the streets as acid. It is still considered one of the most powerful hallucinogen available today. The drug radically alters a person's mental state by distorting the perception of reality. Even doses as minute as twenty-five micrograms — the equivalent of a few grains of salt — will cause hallucinations to occur.

The need for intoxicating stimulants is not a phenomenon confined to the twentieth century. The Celts had their mead, while the Greeks and Romans consumed limitless quantities of wine prior to the days of Christ. Records of intoxicants are part of China's culture as far back as

3000 BC; India and Egypt are not far behind at 2500 BC and 2000 BC respectively. Early explorers like Columbus learned of cocaine along with tobacco from the South America natives. The Spanish introduced cannabis to Chile in 1545, and the plant became a staple crop of colonial farmers. The Jamestown settlers brought the plant to Virginia in 1611, and it was a major crop throughout North America until after the Civil War. Even straight-laced George Washington cultivated it at Mount Vernon in 1765. In 1884, Sigmund Freud dissolved cocaine in water and injected it. He wrote, "A small dose lifted me to the heights in a wonderful fashion."

Drug use is recognized as a sign of moral degeneration, causing governments to enact laws and inflict punishment to control it. Science has shown, however, that both intoxication and addiction reach beyond moral issues. Animals have sought ways to alter their consciousness since the beginning of time. Cows consume locoweed until they lose all sense of equilibrium, cats reach the same state with catnip, birds gravitate toward fermenting fruit, and the list goes on. Intoxication has been a human drive not unlike hunger, thirst and sex, for as long as records have been kept. In his book, Sobering Dilemma, Douglas Hamilton wrote, "For better or worse, people feel driven to alter their consciousness, and attempts to legislate on such matters create a dilemma worse than the one the lawmakers were trying to solve in the first place."

By the early 1970s, lawmakers in Canada and the United States were doing their best to stay ahead of the never-ending variety of natural substances and synthetic derivatives prepared by those seeking a new high or a heightened religious awareness. The resourcefulness of those insisting on getting high was remarkable. When one hallucinogen was outlawed, another took its place.

After LSD came less-powerful copycat drugs with names like mescaline, psilocybin (magic mushrooms), PCP (phencyclidine) and MDA (3,4-Methylenedioxyphenylisopropylamine). Today, even more derivatives of the latter have made their debut, adding to the already ample buffet of designer drugs. MDMA, or Ecstasy as it is known on the streets, is one of the more recent.

Once the novelty of hard-core drugs had run its course by the late 1960s and early 70s, the ride of choice was 3, 4 Methylenedioxyphenyl-isopropylamine, known at street level as MDA or the Love Drug. With them came a laissez-faire attitude towards the use and trafficking of designer drugs. No one was forced to be a user therefore public apathy prevailed. These new hybrid rides were considered non-addictive, and there was minimal loss of life from their misuse. In contrast to the treatment of people using their hard-core relatives, the judicial system levied a slap on the wrist for the first offence. Wasting precious court time on hybrids was not a priority.

Prior to the 1970s, MDA was a quiet social drug for an elite minority of intellectuals. With the new decade, drugs of this nature evolved into a multimillion-dollar business. Cocaine fought its way across the Latin American borders to feed the hungry dragon to the north, while MDA grew out of the cooking pots of urban labs. A college diploma was helpful but not essential. Enormous bankrolls were no longer the prerequisite to getting started in the business of manufacturing or distribution. While MDA was more complicated to make than others, all the necessary ingredients could be found at the local pharmacy or off the shelves of the nearest hardware store. The mega-cartels reluctantly took a back seat to the local ma-and-pa operations.

While MDA was new to the general public as a social aid to personal pleasure, it was no stranger behind the closed doors of government labs. It had been developed in the early twentieth century with the use of public funds and given to Allied soldiers during combat as an appetite depressant or an energy booster. There is a long and checkered history concerning the use and abuse of MDA; not all the use was medical or all the abuse social.

American bio-ethicist Jonathan Moreno wrote in his book *Undue Risk* that, in the early 1950s, private clinics looked to the US military for financial aid. To gain that support, they had to sell their souls to Uncle Sam. The trade-off demanded that they conduct a series of experiments on human guinea pigs, as dictated by their overseers within the US military. While these hospitals and private clinics are founded on the principles of the Hippocratic oath, that is, to offer safe havens to those in need of medical care and to do no harm, a US military internal memo of 1951 expressed a desire to employ them to "investigate the utilization of phychochemical agents both for offensive use and for the protection against them." The question of morality was more loaded than a sailor on shore leave.

In 1953, a New York Psychiatric Hospital received a grant along with a vial containing an unproven agent pulled from the US military's Edgewood Arsenal, labeled EA-1298. Upon receipt of the potion, hospital physicians donned their rubber gloves, put on respiratory masks and followed the enclosed directions by administering the product MDA, in incremental doses to Howard Blauer, an innocent tennis pro who had admitted himself to the facility in a state of acute depression. Blauer knew he was being treated, but he didn't know the treatment was not designed to help him. The institute's contract with the military stated that the objective was "to perfect a form of truth serum" or incapacitating agent. The hospital reported that, "under the supervision of several physicians at the New York State Psychiatric Institute, a series of injections of MDA, with the encoded number EA–1298, were administered to Blauer." After extensive experimentation in which the physicians monitored changes in Blauer's disposition, they were forced to acknowledge just how badly such experiments can turn out. To Blauer's misfortune, his caregivers concluded that 500 milligrams of MDA was lethal.

Alexander Shulgin test-drove MDA in 1969 and reported on its effect at various doses in his book *Phenethylamines I Have Known and Loved*. After consuming 100 milligrams, he stated that: "The coming on was gradual and pleasant, taking from an hour to an hour and a half to do so. The trip was euphoric and intense despite my having been naturally depleted from a working day."

Knowing the effect 500 milligrams had on Howard Blauer, Shulgin put a ceiling on his experiment at 200 milligrams. This new ride "initially brought on nausea within a half hour, followed by a state of stoned intoxication which was very delightful. This lasted for roughly eight hours, leaving a feeling that my judgment was clouded sufficiently that driving of a car was totally out of the question."

Government exploitation of citizens as ignorant specimens for scientific research did not happen only in the United States. In *One Man's Justice*, the autobiography of Thomas Berger, former Supreme Court judge for British Columbia, Thomas tells how he scored a significant victory against the Canadian federal government on behalf of a young girl who, when committed to a Canadian psychiatric clinic, was subjected to several experiments without her consent, all of them financed by and conducted on behalf of the US Central Intelligence Agency. No matter how unconstitutional the procedure, the grant money that accompanied the drugs to be tested tended to cloud the moral conscience of the participating institutions. By some odd twist of fate, MDA eventually found its way onto the shelves of pharmacies throughout Canada and the US during the 1960s as an appetite depressant.

It was not until November 26, 1969, that the Canadian Food and Drug Authority (FDA) rendered it illegal to sell or import MDA. The act of possession however had been carelessly overlooked. Another oversight was the fact that the law makers neglected to amend the Narcotic Control Act in the same manner, leaving any defense a large hole through which to escape prosecution.

There are about twenty different synthetic routes in the preparation of MDA, but the principal component that was used in the local scene was Isosafrole. Though a natural oil extract from the anise seed or sassafras, its less cynical domain in life was as a fragrance in perfumes and soap and as a certified killer of lice. Safrole is one of the oils known as one of the Ten Essential Amphetamines. While designed for use as a fragrance in cosmetics and perfumes, it is a substance not to be handled carelessly. Undue exposure can damage the liver and kidneys and severely poison the thyroid gland. Minor contact will affect respiration and irritate the skin and eyes.

While the recipe for MDA is somewhat laborious, any backyard chemist can pull the ingredients together with minimal difficulty. With a little practice, amateurs can produce a saleable product. The recipe is widely broadcast on the Internet for all to see, and the method of manufacturing MDA has, since the beginning of time, consisted of a four-step procedure. The first step is the production of Ketone, which is the starting material, and this is where the demand for Isosafrole plays a significant role.

The seventies saw some cooperation between the Canadian and US drug enforcement agencies. On June 21, 1972, the RCMP drug division of Windsor, Ontario, received a query from the US Bureau of Narcotics and Dangerous Drugs (predecessor of the US DEA) based in Detroit. At that time, there were three major suppliers of raw chemicals on the east coast. Though the raw materials served as elements in everyday household chemicals, when blended with other solutions, they produced illicit drugs like those previously mentioned. Members of the bureau spent their days scanning the ledgers of each factory, tracing the path of every suspicious purchase.

One such acquisition took them across the Canadian border, where their authority ended abruptly. Per the US agency's query, the British Columbia Institute of Mycology had placed an order for four twenty-five pound containers of 1, 2 Methylenedioxy, 4 – propenyl, commonly known as Isosafrole. The chemical supplier was Matheson, Coleman & Bell of Norwood, Ohio.

The destination on the waybill was 10910 Westdowne Road, Ladysmith, British Columbia, and the consignee was Arthur Williams.

Word on the street at the time suggested that Williams had been honing his skills in the development of MDA as early as 1969 but to the authorities it was undocumented hearsay. If Williams had indeed become involved, the police were in the dark as to where he gained his fundamental training in chemistry. The hippies living on his land may have promoted the idea, but their lifestyle was still a long way from the art of manufacturing.

One source suggested Williams had contacted a radical chemist out of eastern Canada, while another pointed the finger at an American engineer who had taken up a teaching position in Nanaimo. The most interesting theory came from a man who worked alongside Williams as he developed his famous Williams' bow. He states that while Williams was experimenting with his own formula of resin hardener he became intoxicated by the fumes. Thinking the experience was not altogether unpleasant, he wrote the formula down for future reference. According to this trusted friend, "It was that formula that paved the way to his manufacturing MDA." As strange as it may seem, there is a hint of this story's truth in handwritten documents seized from Williams' home during a 1973 raid.

Stanley Cross on the other hand, stated that the MDA was the creation of a fellow known as Chief. "That was the only name I ever heard for him. He was a chemical engineer and lived in the cabin at the front of the Williams' property which Margaret later used for her small business. He had given the formula to Williams, but when he got wind that Art was going into production, this guy packed his bags and hit the road, never to be heard from again."

Shirley Ferguson remembers the Chief as Ron. "He was a native fellow from Ontario and lived in the cabin out front of our place with Gordon Loomis after Gordon had separated from Ruth. He was well educated and did the odd bit of carpentry work for Art. He may have been with Art when he found the formula, but he never gave it to him. Art would spend hours at the University of British Columbia in Vancouver combing the reference books in their library. That's where he found the formula."

Williams' long-time friend Ralph Harris, a fellow immersed in the drug culture stated: "The MDA recipe was originally a 1932 German recipe and Gordon Loomis got it for Art from the UBC library."

So many authorities, all with conflicting memories, but regardless of how he gained his knowledge, there was one thing for certain: if Williams took on such a project, his heart and soul would be poured into making it as good as it could get.

CHAPTER 6:

THE RANK AND FILE

Art was up to no good long before I met him. We hit it off right from the start...

—Dale Stuart Elliott

At 38 years of age, Dave Staples was a strapping man at 6-foot-2 inches and a veteran in the Organized Crime Division having literally rewritten the syllabus for training those on a Drug Squad. On June 21, 1972, Staff Sgt. Staples, the lead man for the Drug Enforcement Division of the Royal Canadian Mounted Police in Victoria, British Columbia, received a memo from his Ottawa counterpart.

Under his direction, a handful of men and women crowded into a 700-square-foot room at the rear of a single-story building located at the corner of Fort and Vancouver streets. As many as sixteen uniformed officers shared a couple of phones, an insufficient number of desks, plus a single stapler.

Staples said, "When the June 21, 1972, memo arrived, we were already working to establish the point of origin for what we saw as a flood of MDA leaching out of the Ladysmith area and flowing as far east as Winnipeg,

Manitoba." In those days, the West Coast was becoming the K-Mart for designer drugs. Staples' division had their hands full with the explosion of synthetic drugs making their way into the universities and onto the city streets. While there were a number of want-a-be chemists who threatened a naïve few with their experiments, there was at least one out there that deserved center stage in a Broadway performance. His product rivaled all others and seemed to only get purer as the months dragged on.

Ladysmith was a scant forty-five miles north of Victoria, but Staples' limited budget and manpower dictated that he had to be certain his men were not driving off on a whim. Though brief and to the point, the source memo requested their assistance to verify the legitimacy of Williams' Institute of Mycology and confirm its declared purpose before ruling out the possibility it was involved in illicit activity. If indeed the chemicals Williams had purchased were to be used in the manufacturing of synthetic drugs, they concluded their likely purpose was in the production of MDA. If their suspicion proved valid, this was no small acquisition for it would eventually yield forty-five pounds of pure MDA or 240,000 capsulated trips.

As a rule, police anti-drug units don't put the big picture together. They are geared to carry out seizure and interdiction because they have a public impact. Agents are rewarded by the volume of drugs and money seized, which fosters a body-count mentality, an unsophisticated rush to see who can put the most powder on the table at press time. It's exciting, highly visible, and it's guaranteed to garner time on the six o'clock news. It shows the taxpayers what they are getting for their money. But with Dave Staples' division, every seizure was part of a much larger enterprise. The arrests they made might allow them to seize twenty capsules in a plastic bag here and twenty more over there, and this would happen repeatedly. But that is where the differences lie between Staples and the beat cops.

Staples and his team exploited each arrest in an attempt to move closer to the source, slowly making their way from the user on the street, to the people who collected the money, to those who wholesaled the drugs, to those who handled the shipping and eventually on to those at the top of the food chain who masterminded the manufacturing. Dave Staples' group did not hunt drugs; it hunted flesh. As conspiracy laws specify, ignorance of the crime nor distance from it, diminishes responsibility.

The problem that Staples faced was that those in the political arena would rather see the nickel-bag dealers paraded before the TV cameras than invest thousands of man-hours combing the back alleys to foster informants needed to serve up a solid case on the source. The politicians simply don't have the patience for a serious game of chess. They make all the right gestures, but as soon as the man-hours start mounting up, they pull the plug on the financial purse strings.

As the Mounties' investigation got underway that June day, they were surprised to discover the BC Institute of Mycology was not yet in their database (the incorporation documents had been submitted to the Register of Titles only nine days earlier), but one thing was for certain: if Arthur James Williams was involved, there is every likelihood it warranted further investigation.

Williams had been apprehended once before, in 1968 on a minor drug offence. The charge of possession of hash had arisen when one of the RCMP liaisons in India tracked a hardcover book from that country to a Ladysmith address. While that, in and of itself was not unusual, the liaison told the Victoria RCMP that the pages of the book had been glued together and the interior had been hollowed out to create a compartment large enough to hide a quantity of the high-grade product. When the package arrived at Ladysmith, the Victoria RCMP lay in wait until Williams marched in, cleaned out his post office box and returned home. The RCMP followed him to his residence on Westdowne Road and waited to confirm that his home was the destination for the package. They needed to be certain that he wasn't merely the courier for someone else.

Art Williams was born with a sixth sense and did everything he could to insure he never silenced his instincts. When he arrived home, he had a premonition that something wasn't right. He left the neatly wrapped package on the dash of his truck, thinking he would retrieve it in the morning if his suspicions proved wrong. As it turned out, he didn't have to wait long. Within minutes of arriving home, two members of the

RCMP drug squad drove onto his property, knocked on his door and demanded to know where the drugs were.

"What drugs?" Williams responded.

"The ones you just picked up at the post office," was the reply.

"You must be referring to that package that was in my post box. I have no idea what is in it, but it's on the dash of my truck. For all I know it could be full of bullshit."

At that moment, the cops knew they didn't have a case but felt they had no option but to pursue it to the end. As expected, Williams appeared before the Nanaimo County Court for a matter of minutes before the judge resolved that the case was built on inconclusive evidence. Since Williams had not taken the package into his home, nor had he opened it, there was nothing to support the claim that he was knowingly in possession of a controlled substance.

The case was dismissed but the RCMP continued to keep an eye on him. They were leery of his anti-authoritarian attitude and, while they were unable to link Williams to the drug trade, he was associated with Dale Elliott, and the latter had been seen in the company of a few men actively engaged in trafficking narcotics throughout the Pacific Northwest.

Dale Elliott was born December 13, 1937, in Saskatoon, Saskatchewan, the eldest of four siblings. His father was a chronic alcoholic with a reputation as a real scrapper when he was liquored up. He always wore a new shirt because the old one would get torn and bloodied from the bar brawl the night before. The owner of a black-market auto dealership, Dale's father would buy cars and trucks at the best price he could find and then transport them to the cities up north, where he would get a much higher price for them. Dale wouldn't see too much of the old man during that time, because he was always away wheeling and dealing.

Dale dropped out of school during grade nine because, in his own words, "I realized I already knew everything they were trying to teach me." After dropping out, he started working for the local farmers. By the time he was fifteen, he had taught himself all phases of gasoline engine rebuilding and was doing overhauls on the farmers' personal vehicles plus their tractors and combines. When he turned seventeen he saw himself having two options: he could stay with the thirty-dollar-a-month job he had or he could enlist in the Canadian Army.

Elliott served Canada as a peacekeeper from the fall of 1957 through 1961 in Germany with the First and Second Battalions of the Queen's Own Rifles. At the convenience and expense of our government, he received formal instruction in the use of weapons and physical hostility. As a sniper, he could put down a six-inch group from 600 yards. But because he refused to follow every order, he was constantly up before his commanding officer and being demoted to a lesser rank. So, it only made sense to Elliott to keep two uniforms in his locker: one a corporal's; the other a rifleman's.

While in Europe, Elliott rode a Triumph 500cc motorcycle as a dispatch rider, a job he liked. "The sergeant-major," he said, "would ask me to take a message somewhere and then want to know exactly how long it would take me. I would say, ten minutes, to which he would respond 'no way.' The route was a mess, with stumps and tank tracks to negotiate, but I made it in the time I stated. I would run that sucker full out through the brush and half the time skip trenches in the air. I found out later the sergeant-major was waging bets on his dispatch riders and I was making him a load of money."

While in Germany, Dale Elliott met Ingrid Marlies Scholven, a native of Hohenlimburg, a small town in the Ruhr Valley. After a short interlude, they decided to get married, but according to a strict internal policy, he first required written permission from his commanding officer. As Elliott suspected, his superior said 'no', but he went ahead and married her anyway. Dale earned his superior's wrath once again in the form of a demotion. Rank and therefore status within the forces meant nothing to Dale, hence the demotions had no effect. Following an honorable discharge from the Royal Canadian Army in 1962, Dale and Ingrid settled in Ladysmith, B.C.

To those who monitored his comings and goings, he left the impression he paid his bills as a self-made mechanic and expert welder, but the police maintained that his primary source of income came from his association with the 101 Knights and the other organized biker gangs that beat the asphalt up and down Vancouver Island.

Elliott was eager to make his statement in that society. The colors he wore on his back testified that he had earned his bones through some form of aggression, and like those he hung with, he lived as hard as he rode. To do time behind bars was to demonstrate the ultimate commitment he and his peers were prepared to endure on behalf of the club, their surrogate family.

There were several biker gangs back then vying for a piece of the Island's turf. The Satan's Angels, the Gypsy Wheelers and the Bounty Hunters were all given options to either close-up shop by the 101 Knights or if individually they represented a suitable candidate, to patch over. One by one the smart members faded back into society. The remainder either adopted the 101 Knights colors or faced harsh consequences.

Prior to the early 1960s, the only criminal force to be reckoned with on the Island was the Mafia, small in number, maintaining a low profile. The 101 Knights had their roots in Powell River on the mainland, north of Vancouver. Sensing an opportunity to prosper, they inched their way onto the Island and pushed the old boys aside. This new breed of crime family had little regard for protocol or diplomacy. They relied on sheer muscle to take out anyone who would not willingly step aside.

By the time Elliott met Williams in 1970, he was a fair-haired, blue-eyed, thirty-four-year-old who tipped the scales at roughly 160 pounds. Those who had the disadvantage of getting to know his aggressive side found in short order that most of his body weight was made up of street-hardened brawn. Unlike many of those he associated with, he wore his hair neatly trimmed and remained, for the most part, clean-shaven. He knew how to party with the best of them, but when circumstances turned ugly, the wise man would give him some distance. In a formal environment, Elliott could hold his own without resorting to vulgarity, but to those who knew him on a personal level, the latter was definitely his area of comfort.

According to Elliott, he and Williams met when a guy who went by the name of Chiefy was rebuilding the engine of a six-wheeled amphibious vehicle for Art and he couldn't get it started. Elliott was known about the area as a wrench who could fix just about anything, so Art asked him to help. "As it turned out, they had put the connecting rod bearing caps in backwards, causing the rods to jam up inside the cylinder sleeves. I just took them out, hit the locking tab with a punch, put them back in and it fired right up."

"Art was up to no good long before I met him," Elliott would say. "We hit it off right from the start and although there never appeared to be a pecking order, I would refer to him as Hauptmann, which is 'top man' or 'Captain' in German." Elliott showed respect for Williams' high level of intelligence and Art repaid that with a trusted friendship. "Art was the most imaginative, unpredictable member of the organization. We worked together, played together and watched each other's back."

Dave Staples, RCMP
Credit: Dave Staples

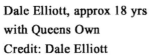

Dale Elliott, approx 18 yrs
with Queens Own
Credit: Dale Elliott

Ingrid Elliott 17 yrs
Credit: Dale Elliott

Dale & Ingrid's wedding
in Germany
Credit: Dale Elliott

101 Knights early 1960's
Credit: Dale Elliott & Fred Wally

CHAPTER 7:

THE DRUGS ARE IN
THE CUPBOARD!

[Williams] had more nerve than a toothache.

—Dave Staples

The fact that Elliott kept police scanners in his truck and mobile home only raised further suspicion that he saw a need to shield his activities from prowling eyes. He and Williams had jointly purchased the property on Old Cowichan Lake Road from Elliott's brother-in-law, Ray Rierson, on August 21, 1971, for $13,000. Elliott moved into the original trailer on the property with Ingrid and their children. Rierson stated, Williams was interested in the property for its soil.

Soon after taking possession of the property, Rierson and another guy helped Elliott frame up a two-story structure which he was going to use as a shop on the main, with living quarters above. He would never get around to finishing the building, but he got it to the point where he could use the shop and his boys took over the upstairs as a place to hang out with their friends.

By 1973 the Elliott's sons had become well-known to the local authorities for "mischief, use of abusive language and assaults against their peers." Numerous letters from concerned parents, plus a petition from an immediate neighbor found their way onto the desk of the local RCMP. Their school principal summed up their antics as "incorrigible." In no time, they were introduced to Les Reid, a probation officer, who concluded that the "anti-social attitude" of their father had "rubbed off" on them.

Dale Elliott's brother Cary, who went by the name of Boots, also felt the need to push the limits of the law. Art Williams' friend Hap Laffin recalls, "This guy would steal anything if it wasn't nailed down, plus he was known about town as a 'torch for hire.' I was told he would gladly torch his own mother's home if he thought it would pay. He was one hell of a tough longshoreman though, and one day he walked onto a ship sitting at berth in Crofton and went straight into the captain's quarters, where he picked up the captain's Zeiss binoculars and walked out with them under his arm as bold as brass."

The RCMP noticed another man in Williams' company who popped up on their radar. Raymond Albert Ridge was a warm-hearted fellow toward those he trusted but tough toward all others. He tipped the scales at a hair over 200 pounds, standing six feet two inches tall. His expression was generally stern. He had a barrel chest, and his arms filled the sleeves of his T-shirt, leaving those who wanted to challenge him thinking twice. The tattoo decorating his right forearm spoke of his philosophy of life: a dagger piercing a heart, with the script beneath it reading "Death Before Dishonor." His black hair was neatly trimmed and he was normally clean-shaven except for short sideburns and a moustache that clung to his upper lip. According to a number of people who knew him personally, he was a man you paid serious attention to. As far as the authorities could tell, he filled his days working as a chokerman for local logging operations. As for his off hours, the RCMP could only surmise.

Ray Ridge was a mere kid when Art Williams first laid eyes on him. Williams had paid the Ridge family a visit and quickly realized that

Ray and his younger brother David were lacking a parental figure not associated with physical abuse. For reasons, which later proved obvious, Williams took them under his wing, and as a result they thought the world of their mentor. In no time their blind allegiance proved worthy of every minute he invested.

Ray Ridge was born in Central Butte, Saskatchewan, on April 30, 1947. By the time he had celebrated his fifteenth birthday, their parents had abandoned him and his brother to their own resources. By the time the cops started paying close attention to Williams and his activities, Ridge was twenty-five years, and not only willing, but able, to be molded and conditioned into a loyal foot soldier.

Ridge's ex-wife, Bev Nicholls recalled, "Art ruled both the boys as peons. He told them what to do, and as with everyone else in his life, his way was the only way." Both Ray and David had a capacity for violence, and while Art didn't support such behavior, when necessary he was cunning enough to use the threat of it to his advantage." Ray was no saint, and he saw the inside of a prison cell without Williams' involvement when he was convicted in June 1971 of trafficking, assault and a weapons offence.

As the investigation into Williams expanded, so did their concern that something was terribly out of sync with the picture they uncovered. Under cover of darkness, a handful of men led by Dave Staples snuck onto Williams' property during the first week of July 1972 with hopes of defining their target's objective. They moved forward as cautiously as they could, not wishing to alert Art of their presence or leave telltale signs they had been snooping around his property. Information they had received earlier suggested there were lookout towers and trip-wire booby traps surrounding the perimeter of the property, and this only reinforced their need for slow and careful movement.

A few months earlier a conservation officer for the Department of Fisheries and Wildlife had tripped a hidden security wire while considering the damage caused by a beaver dam on the property immediately west of Williams' land. Within minutes he was face to face with a group of tattooed bikers who demanded to know what business he had on their land.

Staples was surprised to discover the barn-like structure that had recently been erected on Williams' property and that it was more like a fortress than an institution of nutritional discovery. Massive pieces of wood, four inches thick had been laminated together and secured as the exterior doors. Locks were arranged along the jam of the main door with such complexity and of such a design that the officers were left puzzled and without the ability to enter. Standing like sentries at the opposing corners of the five acres were the twin towers he had been told of and by all appearance they served as outposts to monitor the comings and goings from his land.

Approaching the problem from a different angle, the RCMP canvassed chemical supply houses in Vancouver and Toronto in September 1972. They found three doing business with the BC Institute of Mycology. Williams had placed a large order for laboratory equipment with one of them. The police felt confident there was more going on in Williams' life than his development of a hybrid mushroom.

With no idea what he would find, Dave Staples instructed another member of his team, Sergeant Gerry O'Neill to carry out a second covert raid on the large BC Institute of Mycology's lab. O'Neill had with him a member of the RCMP bomb squad to deal with the detonation devices rumored to litter the place.

To their surprise the main door of the lab was unlocked. Beyond the entrance, they passed through a small foyer that led directly into the principal portion of the facility. The place was so clean you could eat off the floors. Every piece of equipment had its place, and large air filters were built into the wall to ensure that any and all contaminants were contained before they reached the clean lab environment. Ultraviolet lighting hung everywhere, offering a superb growing environment for the mushroom spores.

All the freshwater taps were equipped with purifiers, and the heating was thermostatically controlled using hot-water radiators that again reduced the circulation of dust particles. O'Neill uncovered nothing on his visit, so the drug squad could only wait until the word on the street hinted that production had gathered momentum.

A few weeks earlier, on August 24, the shipment of Isosafrole that had alerted US and Canadian agencies to Williams' activities arrived at the warehouse of Canadian Pacific Transport in Nanaimo, twenty-four miles north of Ladysmith. Dave Staples drove to the CP Transport office in advance and etched his initials on the inside bottom rim of each of the four barrels for future identification.

On the day the barrels were released, he played the part of a shipping clerk and watched a man who identified himself as A.W. Williams take receipt of the four barrels and load them into a pickup truck with the assistance of his friend Stanley Cross. Upon leaving the warehouse, Staples had Williams followed by four officers in four unmarked vehicles. They jockeyed their position so not one of them stayed within eyeshot of Williams' car for longer than absolutely needed. Williams made his way to a Ladysmith restaurant, stayed there no more than five minutes and then proceeded on down the road to the government liquor store and to Stanley Cross's home, where he stayed till early evening. After that he returned home to Westdowne Road.

Unaware that Williams was being watched at the CP warehouse, his associates Terry Quinn and Lou Brown had driven to the Nanaimo RCMP headquarters at 203 Prideaux Street. While Williams was loading his four barrels, the pair boldly sauntered through the RCMP parking lot, writing down the license numbers of every vehicle, private and otherwise, marked or unmarked. Corporal Eastham stood inside the building and watched through the tinted windows. To Eastham it appeared Williams was doing his best to taunt the RCMP. From his vantage point, he could see Lou Brown's red Sunbeam Alpine parked across the road with two barrels identical to those at the CP warehouse, rising above the rear seat. Eastham immediately contacted Staples to tell him what was going on and that it appeared Williams had already picked up the shipment. Staples assured Eastham that he was still watching the pickup of the barrels unfold within the warehouse. Williams' attempted diversion didn't work, but Staples gave him an "A" for his effort.

There were other events and each made the authorities more suspicious, but they found no evidence that the chemicals were being used for anything other than legitimate research to produce a better mushroom. They knew it would take time and a vigilant watch to prove otherwise.

Staples believes Williams must have questioned the number of times the same nondescript grey sedan sat just off to the side of his Westdowne Road driveway. He had to have noticed the lone occupant squirming about the driver's seat each time he or one of his cronies left the property. But he carried on with his activities as if it didn't matter.

Dave Staples adds, "He had more nerve than a toothache. All the time we were watching him and unbeknownst to us, he was tuned into one of our seven radio frequencies. We found out later that Williams had purchased radio scanners to outfit his lab, house and car and knew every move we made with enough time to cover his tracks."

Staples uncovered freight records that showed Williams had received lab equipment and chemicals each month from March through September 1972. When two bulky requisitions arrived from Central Scientific Company of Canada and Fisher Scientific Company of Vancouver, Staples was confident they deserved a closer look. In themselves they would have drawn no interest, but in light of the original Isosafrole shipment, all that changed.

With the cooperation of Loomis Courier Services, Sergeant Edward Malinowski of the Nanaimo RCMP General Investigation Section (GIS) took the containers from the warehouse to his detachment headquarters, where he permanently engraved each item with a carbon-tip marking pencil. Some pieces were marked with the officer's enlistment number, 18510; others with a sideways "M," or "lazy M" as the cops referred to it, resting against an "E"; and others with a "T" or a simple "+" stenciled across the head of a screw or in an inconspicuous location around the neck of a flask or beneath the lip of a lid.

Williams somehow got wind of their interference, and when he arrived to pick up his acquisition he flew into a rage. Leaving the warehouse, he stood outside and watched the clerk through the window. Not content to leave it there, Williams commenced legal action against the transport company for breach of contract, and before he dropped his action against them, he did everything within his power to insure it had cost the firm dearly in legal fees.

On October 3, 1972, Williams rode the ferry to Vancouver to collect another of his orders. Richard Logan, an undercover officer for the RCMP, met him at the shipping warehouse looking much like one of the hired help and entered trivial conversation. His goal was to entrap Williams by implying that he knew what he was up to and could satisfy his appetite for a continuous flow of chemicals if he so desired. But Williams was not the fool they took him for. He left the warehouse, drove around just long enough to gather his wits and then returned to inform the office manager that he had better keep an eye on Logan. He stated that the man was either a crook or a member of the drug squad.

At 9:20 a.m. on October 24, 1972, Williams once again arrived at the CP Transport office in Nanaimo. Lou Brown was at the wheel of his 1961 Sunbeam Alpine sports car, while Terry Quinn straddled the console and Williams wedged into the passenger seat. Their task was to take receipt of four additional tins of Isosafrole.

Staples had preceded Williams to the transport company's office and once again marked all the containers with his initials. He made a copy of the manifest and discovered the shipment originated from the same supplier, in Ohio, as the previous Isosafrole delivery. Staples and two of his buddies waited patiently in a camper parked in the company's lot. As one man snapped photographs as evidence, Staples observed that Williams did not take delivery of the containers at that time. Even if he had wished to take the shipment home with him, there was no way he could squeeze the four containers into the sports car along with its passengers. At 4:40 that afternoon, Williams returned with Stanley Cross's pickup and loaded his cargo.

On July 4, 1973, RCMP corporal Gary Thomas, a member of Nanaimo's General Investigative Section (GIS), intercepted a box at Loomis Armored Car Service in Nanaimo. It contained a Cenco heating mantel, addressed to Williams' Institute of Mycology. Thomas returned the package to the Loomis office for delivery on July 6.

In August, a third shipment of four tins of Isosafrole arrived from the same Ohio company. It cleared customs as "fungicide." Over the following three months the RCMP intercepted a total of eleven shipments of chemical apparatus, scales, beakers and glassware of various sizes.

Stanley Cross shared, "I got along well with Art as he was an awesome guy to be around. He put me to work and gave me the title 'Production Manager' for the Institute of Mycology. Art was pretty proud of the name he came up with for the business and he even had business cards printed with my name on them. He paid me very well but it was always in cash. Art carried a big roll of bills around with him. When he was in the presence of the cops or any other form of authority he would flash the wad just to see how they'd react. He always put the larger bills on the top to give the impression he was loaded. He could bullshit most everyone and scare the bejesus out of them, but not me.

"Part of my job was to pick up some of the shipments from the freight warehouse. If it was late in the day, I would take them home with me and leave them in my truck with instructions to deliver them to Art the following morning. I knew the cops had been keeping an eye on me because I was working with them on another case, so when they came over early in the morning, I wasn't overly surprised. I guess they wanted to verify that the shipment that I had on my truck was the one they had seen at the Transport warehouse. You can imagine how disturbed they were and surprised I was when we discovered it wasn't. The RCMP immediately accused me of tampering with the evidence and trying to frustrate their investigation. I assured them that I had left the chemicals in the back of the truck the night before, and the only possibility I could think of was that Art had come over during the night and swapped the barrels."

"Art was brilliant at manipulation and had a classic way of setting people up," says Ruth Loomis. Williams knew the police had cameras trained on his property from the trailer park next door. Often Hap Laffin would tell Williams that he had been stopped by friends who were members of the RCMP and told, "I saw you on the cameras yesterday." Over time it became a choreographed sequence of movements that would yield nothing more than a list of those who came and went on the property. Those who Williams wanted to protect would simply arrange to meet him elsewhere.

"Art Williams knew we had his phone tapped," said Dave Staples. "He would use coded sentences like 'Your alpha meal is ready,' or 'Your alfalfa breakfast is in the cupboard.' We didn't have the sophisticated equipment at our disposal that we have today. Nevertheless, there wasn't the stringent legislation in place to deal with such matters so it was a lot easier back then to tap a phone.

We made up little transistors with alligator clips and we'd hike ourselves up a pole opposite the Williams' home and clamp onto his phone line and then set ourselves up in a co-operative home or garage across the road where we taped his conversations. There was no such thing as a number recorder to log whomever Williams or his cronies were calling, so we rigged one up out of a household doorbell. We removed the bell and attached a number 25-syringe needle to the end of the clanger. We ran a spool of adding-machine paper past the needle, and as he dialed a number, the telephone pulse would punch holes into the paper equal to the numerical digit he called. All we had to do was read it backwards and we knew whom he was calling. It was crude but effective."

Art Williams' sister Gladys recalls, "Art stopped in at our place in Sherwood Park, Alberta, on the way back from one of his trips to Germany and phoned Margaret. Margaret told him 'the drugs were in the cupboard.' He laughed and said the silly buggers would believe anything they hear. There is no doubt he knew his phone had been tapped."

Dale Elliott's home
Credit: Vancouver Appeals Court

Dale's workshop adjacent home
Credit: Vancouver Appeals Court

Ray Ridge
Credit: Bev Nichols

Art's mycology lab in barn
Credit: Vancouver Appeals Court

CHAPTER 8:

RULES OF CONDUCT

…they can pop lab after lab and I will remain safe because I never made two of them the same.

—Art Williams

Between June 1972 and September 1973, Sergeant Gerry O'Neill, of Dave Staples' drug squad, surreptitiously entered Dale Elliott's property thirty to forty times, mostly without gaining any information about Elliott's activities. His efforts were thwarted by the German shepherds that guarded the Elliott home, by the flock of domestic geese that roamed the property as sentries and by the sheer number of people coming and going. O'Neill reported the area surrounding his home and workshop was lit at all hours by stadium lighting, making it impossible to approach under the cover of darkness, and rumors that Elliott owned a few rifles, which he kept loaded and would not hesitate to use to protect his privacy, made each visit even more harrowing. As Elliott put it: "The most dangerous gun is an unloaded one".

Those working in drug squads liken their work to climbing a mountain. Both are considered dangerous; both take a long time to complete;

and both endeavors are considered an utter failure unless participants attain their goal. For the RCMP, the goal is identifying those responsible for manufacturing or distributing drugs.

During August 1973, an informant connected to the drug squad directed the cops to a property on Swallowfield Road in Chemainus. He suggested they would find a lab on land Elliott had rented from his brother-in-law, Ray Rieirson. O'Neill entered the site that night with a couple of teammates but left empty-handed when they were unable to gain access to a windowless cabin that was locked up tighter than Fort Knox.

On September 11, O'Neill paid the cabin another late-night visit, this time in the company of an expert locksmith from Vancouver. Even with professional help, it took more than three hours to make the tumblers flow in the right direction. Their timing was off. If it had ever been used as a lab, there was no evidence to support the claim. Elliott later confirmed, "I had a gut feeling the cops were going to be looking at that site. I didn't want my sister and brother-in-law involved so I packed everything up a couple of weeks in advance of their arrival."

At the same time, other members of the force were maintaining surveillance on Elliott's personal residence. When daylight compromised their efforts, they studied aerial photographs of Elliott's land in hopes of spotting a structure that could serve as a laboratory, but nothing jumped out of the black-and-white images. As night returned, they combed the perimeter of his property, staying just outside the range of the floodlights.

Numerous people lived on Elliott's property. In addition to Elliott there was his wife and their five kids, his elderly parents, his brother Boots and several bikers who rented trailers set at strategic points throughout his land. Everyone watched for unwanted visitors, leaving nothing to chance.

Under the direction of Dave Staples, Constable Al Hickman of the Saanich Police crept onto the Elliott property late one evening and hid beneath a bush just a few yards from the entrance to Dale Elliott's home. He hoped to see or overhear something of significance, but not long after he had settled in, Elliott's wife, Ingrid, returned home and parked her car so close to where he was lying that, as he said, he could have whistled the national anthem up her tailpipe. Nervous perspiration poured into his eyes as Ingrid sat and listened to the car radio, totally unaware of his presence. Fortunately, the German shepherds were constrained. An hour passed with Ingrid remaining in the driver's seat, followed by a second and a third painful hour. Had Hickman felt the need to run, his muscles were so seized that he would have been unable to move. In due course, Ingrid left the car, allowing Hickman to make a slow retreat. While nothing landmark came from his visit, it did prove that Elliott's perimeter could be penetrated.

The RCMP continued to visit the property, but Hickman's success at getting close to any of the buildings was the exception rather than the norm. More often they would access the property from the rear after pushing through a mile or more of dense bush. No matter what direction they used to gain access, they couldn't position themselves close enough to get a peek inside Elliott's home. Again, and again they saw nothing more than the trailer's exterior. In the steep terrain of drug investigations, this switchback route is the reason arrests often occur at inchworm speed.

On the evening of September 25, Gerry O'Neill and his partner Constable Bob Bowen were making another approach when they heard a noise that stopped them in their tracks. From the brush, off to the left side of the driveway came a faint humming sound, like the motor of a surveillance camera. Assuming they no longer had cover worth maintaining, they pushed through to the source of the noise and discovered another windowless building not unlike the one on Swallowfield Rd.

They felt they were beginning to see the underbelly of the beast as they had uncovered the mother lode at last. They could hear fans running inside the cabin, and on the far side of the shack an exhaust fan pushed out an odor resembling ripe mothballs. The locks appeared as impregnable and of a more intricate design than those on the Swallowfield Road cabin. Through a tiny crack in the clapboard siding, O'Neill could make out the glow of a single light illuminating a beaker sitting on a workbench and a burner with a pot resting above it.

Long after the RCMP had closed their file, Elliott stated that he and Williams had made the lock using a spring clutch drive and two spring-loaded deadbolts pinpointing a series of holes in the side of the door casing. These connected to cables that ran up through the ceiling and to the outside of the structure. To unlock the door, you needed a quarter-inch rod with an eye in the end. If you worked the rod and pulled the cables at the same time, the tumblers would fall free and the door would move aside on rollers.

Team members maintained a perpetual watch on the shed, staying at the VIP Motel in Duncan between shifts so they did not have to make the round-trip home to Victoria or Nanaimo each day. Staples knew that fatigue could play havoc with this stage of an investigation.

Excursions to Elliott's shed became a daily event although they had no success at penetrating it, even with the aid of a locksmith. Late on the evening of October 10, 1973, Sergeant O'Neill found the lock on the door hanging open. In the company of Constable Bowen, he took eight photographs of the interior.

Although their visit produced no smoking gun, there was no doubt they were in the right place. On a makeshift table sat a flash evaporator, necessary for two of the four stages in producing MDA. Other laboratory equipment was stored in boxes in a back corner of the shed. O'Neill and Bowen marked each of the items with an indelible pen, and, after taking additional photographs for their files, they left the place as they found it.

On October 13, O'Neill and Constable Morrison took a closer look at the cabin on Rieirson's property. Forcing open the door, they found a neatly made bed, table, chest and freezer. O'Neill picked up a couple of pieces of paper from off the floor. One was a hospital bill made out to Dale Elliott and dated May 22, 1973. The other contained what resembled a chemical formula. From the freezer, he collected a small sample of white powder that dusted the bottom. This he sent off to the RCMP Crime Detection Laboratory in Vancouver, for examination by Don Saturley, a civilian member of the RCMP. Saturley oversaw the toxicology section, but after a thorough examination he reported there was no trace of drugs.

On October 17, at 5:30 a.m., O'Neill returned to Elliott's property and once again found the lab door open. Using a hypodermic needle, he took a sample of liquid from a container sitting on the counter. This was sent to the RCMP Crime Lab for examination. A week later the results came back positive for MDA.

O'Neill continued to visit both the Elliott and Rieirson properties, sometimes gaining access and taking photographs, at other times peering through cracks in the wall. Other officers maintained surveillance, recording motor vehicle license numbers and the comings and goings of various people until December 17, 1973.

At last the cops were beginning to realize the fruits of their labor, but they knew that if the case was going to hold up in court, they had to secure more evidence. Every precaution had to be taken to ensure that Williams or Elliott would find no hole in their web through which they could slip free.

For the RCMP, the key was to know when Elliott's cauldrons were beginning to brew. On-site surveillance was not only costly but also a slow means of gathering information when other work cried out for their attention. One option was to plant a bug or series of listening devices in Elliott's residence and the shack that twice sat with its front door open. This became a priority.

During the early days of the investigation into Arthur Williams, there was no law that governed the wiretapping of private phone lines or the use of listening devices in vehicles and on private land. So, in the fall of 1973, drug squad members had no compunction about drilling a small hole into the roof of Elliott's shed and feeding one of their minute radio transmitters into it. There was no physical change to the interior of the building, and unless Elliott or one of his boys crawled onto the roof and removed a couple of shingles, no one would ever be the wiser. The chosen device was so cheap to produce that when the surveillance was over, the RCMP would simply abandon it to the elements rather than risk confrontation.

To insure a clear record of a conversation, the receiver had to be set up within a short distance of the transmitter. This presented a dilemma until Elliott's neighbor, Fred Shiller, received the RCMP's assurance of his personal safety. Shiller granted Staples' crew access to a camper that had been stored on his property directly across Old Lake Cowichan Road from Elliott's driveway. This site offered clear radio reception and an unobstructed view up Elliott's driveway to his trailer. Someone was stationed in the camper twenty-four seven. When the embedded officer saw activity on the property, he would squint from his foxhole and make notes on those who came and went. Regretfully the neighbour's civic-minded decision was also his undoing. When the investigation was finished, Shiller found himself the subject of threats and never-ending harassment from Williams and Elliott's associates. Eventually they forced him to sell his property at a loss and move as far away as his limited funds would permit.

In addition to the camper, unobtrusively dressed men and women, on foot and motorcycles, in cars, vans and delivery trucks, wrapped Williams and his associates in an invisible veil of scrutiny from dawn till dusk, seven days a week. Others huddled in the confines of their office and pored over a river of babble that came from the recorded tapes generated daily by their listening device, searching for a key word, phrase, or pattern. They checked license numbers and combed through phone records, trying desperately to replace rumor with reality as they searched for a fragment of bone that would form part of the skeleton they barely knew.

Just when Dave Staples felt he had a handle on all the players, other matters dictated that he transfer much of the day-to-day investigation to Sergeant Bob Hawkes. Hawkes looked like central casting's version of a narc with his tanned complexion and straight chestnut hair. He was a strapping man, a fraction over six feet tall, with broad shoulders and a stance that made it clear he meant business. His brown eyes were watchful, and while his voice was soft, it remained steady, forcing you to listen to him. Those who know him say he is a hard guy to read, which may have been a determining factor in his success as a cop.

The pressure was now on Hawkes to get up to speed on the investigation, find the source of the MDA and put those individuals out of business. He soon realized that Williams insulated himself as best he could from whatever was going down. From one listening device, Williams' was heard to say, "The cops couldn't prove the equipment I had in the lab was being used to manufacture MDA. I never go to where the stuff is being made, so they can't tie me in, and they can pop lab after lab and I will remain safe because I never made two of them the same. As for the chemicals I kept around my place, they could be used in manufacturing other things."

In early December, the bug started to deliver some worthwhile secrets. During one transmission, Elliott walked into the lab and gave his two boys, aged thirteen and fifteen, hell for not working hard enough. The transmitter not only fed the RCMP verbal reports, but also captured the sound of the fresh brew coming to a boil. This was chased by an automated stirring device with the faint sound of a vacuum in the background.

Don Saturley, the Mounties' civilian chemist, moved into the camper so he could inform Hawkes of the exact moment a new batch of MDA had been completed. The signal Saturley was looking for was the motor of the reflux pump starting up. The pump ran at the final stage in MDA development, when the toxic brew was cleaned of its impurities, it would leave the chemist with a fine paste and the RCMP with the evidence they needed to clinch their case.

At 10 p.m. on December 15, 1973, Hawkes gathered his crew of twenty specialized officers at the Mounties' Nanaimo office to brief them on the plans for the early hours of the following morning. The lead men were Jerry Moloci, Chester Kary, John Abbott, Blaine Froats, John Colliar, Brian Kowalski, Roger Cooper, Doug Morrison, Rolland Goulet and Michael Onischuk. Pat Convey, an expert in explosives and locks, had come over from Vancouver's Security Engineering Division to help clear the path. Rather a tall order for one man, but the easy going, soft spoken Convey put it, "somebody had to do it."

By midnight they were on Elliott's property, waiting for Saturley's signal to proceed.

RCMP evidence photo of Elliott's property
Credit: Vancouver Appeals Court

Swallowfield lab
Credit: Daryl Ashby

Lab on Dale Elliott's property
Credit: Vancouver Appeals Court

Lab on Elliott's property
Credit: Vancouver Appeals Court

Actual recorder RCMP used on Williams and his crew
Credit: Dave Staples

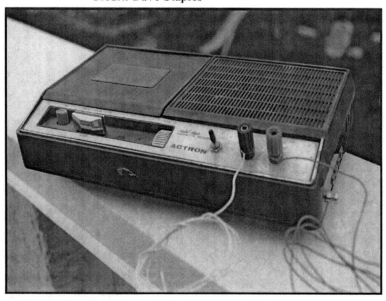

CHAPTER 9:

THE RAID

We felt it was our job to distract the police so that Art could get rid of anything that was incriminating.

—Terry Ferguson

At precisely 1:55 a.m. on December 17, 1973, Morrison and Goulet moved slowly through the bush towards Elliott's lab. They stopped short as they noticed the lab door hung open with two people milling about outside. A single interior light allowed them to see Dale return inside while his son Jerry remained outside with his back to the officers. Thirty seconds passed before Dale returned and kneeled in front of his son. Morrison and Goulet watched as Dale Elliott poured a liquid from one beaker into another as the boy fanned the white cloudy vapors with a small piece of plywood.

"I was mixing formic acid and ammonium hydroxide to make formamide, and it tends to erupt if you don't do it just right," said Dale Elliott. "It's not an explosion, but rather the result of two chemicals getting angry when the process is rushed and agitated."

As Morrison reached the lab he shouted "Police." Startled, Elliott's son recoiled headlong into Morrison's arms. The container fell to the ground, drenching the young boy, Morrison and Goulet, forcing them all to retreat from the fumes. Within seconds, Bob Hawkes and two others were on the scene. Bred to stand his ground, Jerry put up such a struggle that Hawkes had to pin the lad against a log to handcuff him. Both Elliott and his son were taken towards the senior Elliott's trailer and searched. From Elliott's left pants pocket, Morrison seized a ring of keys, one of which Elliott acknowledged would open the lock on the lab.

Don Saturley, the first to enter the lab, confirmed that the two were in the final stages of manufacturing a fresh batch of MDA. Corporal Chester Kary entered a shed near the lab and found three garbage bags containing several empty gelatin capsules. Constable Abbott, who in his civilian life had been a laboratory assistant, took charge of the lab and systematically recorded its contents, leaving all the evidence in place until Sergeant George Eppy of the Nanaimo General Identification Section had taken photographs and measurements to corroborate their findings.

Meanwhile, Constable Froats and three other officers proceeded to Dale Elliott's trailer, entering the front door with guns drawn. Five high-caliber rifles lay on a table near the door along with eight fully loaded clips. Elliott confessed he never kept a gun that wasn't loaded.

Elliott's two youngest boys were sitting on the couch, and ten-year-old Raymond immediately bolted for the door. Froats managed to holster his weapon and grab the lad by the back of his shirt as he darted by and placed him in cuffs. Seven-year-old Mona slept through the whole ordeal on the top bunk in her bedroom. Rather than wake her, Froats wrapped her in a blanket and handed her to one of his fellow officers. The children's mother, Ingrid, was visiting her parents in Germany at the time.

From Dale Elliott's home, Froats retrieved five jars containing crystals, a new radio scanner, and a box containing an Ohaus Dial-O-Gram balance scale. In the hallway, he looked through an apple box containing numerous pieces of paper, including a page of Williams' handwritten notes. The notes dealt with the "method to extract Myristicin from nutmeg." Myristicin gives nutmeg its flavor and odor; it is not analogous to ketone but is associated with Ecstasy, a completely different drug, MMDA.

In the freezer compartment of Elliott's refrigerator, Froats saw quart bottles filled with a brown liquid that gave off a distinct odor he didn't recognize. While searching the children's sleeping area, Froats picked up a toy rubber finger from a cardboard box containing crayons and marking pencils. The finger was about six inches long; within it was a role of paper currency.

Corporal Cooper made his way to the trailer belonging to Elliott's parents, Stuart and Lois. The couple was in bed. Stuart had been sick all day and Lois was in the process of phoning the doctor when the cops burst into the bedroom. According to Stuart, the men told them they were cops, but never showed any form of identification. The couple, both in the nude, were dragged out of bed. Stuart was handcuffed and became agitated when the cops refused to leave the room long enough for Lois to get dressed. In the end, they handed her a robe, but refused to turn around while she put it on.

After searching the couple's bedroom, Cooper discovered a red loose-leaf notebook filled with notations, most of them innocuous except for four pages that contained the recipe for preparing ketone. The old man stated he did not know who owned or wrote in the book and denied knowing of its presence. Sergeant Colliar noticed Stuart Elliott was sweating profusely, and his wife mentioned he had suffered a couple of emphysema attacks that evening and was prone to such attacks when he became excited or nervous.

Behind the trailer was a larger two-story workshop where Elliott and his buddies repaired their motorcycles. The upper level was unfinished but contained some furniture and appeared to be used as transient sleeping quarters. After a thorough search, the police concluded nothing of importance was going to be found there.

In the company of Constable Goulet, Elliott acknowledged that the property was his, as were all the buildings situated on it except for the trailer in which his parents resided. He further stated the laboratory was his. Morrison gave the key to Constable Abbott, who later confirmed it worked properly in the lock.

Dale Elliott and his four boys were placed in one police cruiser while his parents and five-year-old Mona were loaded into a second vehicle. All were driven to the Duncan RCMP headquarters. Stuart and Lois were detained in a separate area while the children were held until temporary foster care could be provided.

Just about the time Hawkes and his boys were wrapping things up, David Clifton McGrath, who was known to the RCMP as a member of the 101 Knights, drove onto the property with a female companion. He spoke briefly to Constable Brian Kowalski then left.

McGrath held a degree of significance in their investigation. Because of a separate investigation, he had been pulled over by the RCMP on July 27, 1972, after leaving Elliott's property. McGrath fled his car and took to the brush adjacent to the road. Following a lengthy chase, he was apprehended, and 197 capsules of MDA were retrieved, leading to his conviction for possession of MDA. Oddly enough, during the raid of Elliott's property, neither Hawkes nor any of his peers considered it beneficial to question him further.

Other than an assorted number of lab utensils, which Williams had clearly purchased, the only link to Williams was a single sheet of paper in Williams' handwriting that turned up in Elliott's hallway closet. The paper contained half of the formula to produce MDA. Hawkes remained optimistic that the second half would be found in Williams' possession providing evidence of the Elliott-Williams conspiracy that they would need for a conviction.

Once the Elliott's were in custody and the property secured, Sergeant Hawkes led his team along Highway 1, fifteen miles north to the Williams residence. At 4:55 a.m., with darkness still working to their advantage, Corporal Kary and Pat Convey broke through Williams' front door with shotguns raised. They were standing over Williams before he could lift his head off his pillow. Sergeant Bob Hawkes showed Williams his badge and told him they were RCMP, they had just arrested Elliott and they had his lab.

Arthur Williams responded with a torrent of profanity that would have shamed a sailor and exhausted the average man, but Art's tirade became more animated and creative as the Mounties moved deeper into one room and then to another.

Pat Convey recalls, "Once Williams had gotten out of bed, I held the shotgun to his face, and I sincerely thought I was going to have to shoot him from the way he was behaving. He told Hawkes that if I didn't remove the shotgun from his house, he was going to take it and shove it up his ass. Stature wise I stood a wee bit taller than Williams at five feet eleven inches, and I weighed in around 170 pounds, but that didn't deter Williams from recoiling like a rattlesnake when you step on its tail. He was completely naked and out of control, leaving me with the feeling that I had no option but to shoot him or keep backing up. I have found that when a man is confronted naked he is most vulnerable and therefore likely to be irrational in the choices he makes."

When Williams finally settled down, he got dressed and voluntarily led the cops to the small lab that was located twenty feet behind his home. As the cops entered the building however, he shook with rage and berated them for wearing their filthy shoes into the building where a sign overhead clearly read "Please remove shoes." His demeanor changed again when they entered a small room behind the workshop, which contained a number of plastic containers. Williams warned the officers not to touch them as it would not be good for their health.

The central portion of the building, which was eight feet wide by ten feet long, clearly functioned as a laboratory and contained bookshelves, a desk, a chair and a filing cabinet. Constable Onischuk sat down in the chair and chatted with the accused about his library. Williams commented proudly that, he "had books that they didn't even have in the University of Victoria library." When Onischuk asked him if he knew everything in the books, Williams walked over to the shelves and replied, "Let me show you something." He pulled out a large book entitled Handbook of Chemistry and Physics, 51st Edition, 1970-71, placed it on the desk in front of Onischuk and opened it, pulling a folded piece of paper from between the pages. He immediately placed the paper against his left thigh, as though he'd had a change of heart and decided he didn't want it to be seen. Hawkes, who was also in the room, saw what had happened and took the paper from Williams' hand. On it was typewritten the two-part formula for manufacturing MDA. Hawkes was stunned that Williams would direct them to the formula when the officers had never mentioned the purpose of the raid. The Crown inferred from this that Williams knew the officers were concerned with MDA and that he had conspired with Elliott in the production of the drug.

Williams commented, "You were going to find it anyway. I might as well help you." Following that act of cooperation, he walked over to the filing cabinet and said, "I'll help you find some more stuff." Sergeant Hawkes replied that he would appreciate any help he could provide, at which point Williams slammed the file drawer closed without producing anything further following which he kicked his verbal tirade back into high gear.

Without Williams' help, Hawkes located a coil binder in the library that contained several pages in the suspect's handwriting, mixed with pages written by someone else. He also found photocopies of scientific articles, descriptions of what were apparently sanctioned experiments with MDA and a number of other hallucinogenic drugs, plus some receipts and invoices made out to Elliott from the Nanaimo Foundry and Engineering Works Ltd., dated August 19, 1971. As Hawkes removed each page, he numbered them in the order taken, but when Saturley examined the evidence later, he found them to be "significantly out of order."

While everything represented evidence of Williams' involvement in the drug culture, nothing proved conclusive as to when he began his experiments. Hawkes knew any activity involving MDA that took place before the Food and Drug Act was amended in 1969 would have been completely legal.

Less than cordial conversation continued between Hawkes and Williams for approximately two hours. Hawkes allowed Williams to wander freely and fix himself a cup of tea. At times Hawkes had no idea where his suspect was or whether any other member of his team had kept an eye on him. All he knew was that during this period the other members of his party were conducting a thorough sweep of the property.

Daniel Ferguson, Shirley's youngest son, remembers, "As kids, Art always told us that cops were bad and he encouraged us to cause them as much grief as we could whenever the opportunity presented itself. During the raid, we were petrified at first, but once we knew what was going on, we just got mad. The cops tried to keep us in our bedrooms while they were going through the house, the shop out back and the grounds for whatever they could find, but we were determined to defy their orders no matter what. If they told us to turn right, we'd turn left. We were swearing like troopers and did our best to get under their skin. The cops were so mad at us that one of them tried to grab Terry, and this caused Art and Shirley to freak out all over again. We were kicking and punching, and Terry managed to get away and crawl under the house. It took three cops to coax him out. Then we both climbed to the top of the tower that Art had built out back of his workshop, where we pelted the cops with rocks. "We felt it was our job to distract the police so that Art could get rid of anything that was incriminating."

Sergeant Eppy photographed the interior of the building and drew a plan of its layout as he did with Elliott's lab. After Saturley had completed his survey, he concluded the principal purpose for the lab was the cultivation of mushrooms. The team left with only the evidence they had collected.

The next afternoon, Sgt. Bob Hawkes and Sgt. John Colliar visited Dale Elliott's parents in their respective Duncan cells and asked each of them if they were prepared to provide a written statement, hinting that their cooperation would help them if the case went to trial.

Lois Elliott held firm to her conviction that the less said the better, even when Sergeant Colliar asked her to explain the ten compromising photographs that he had seized from her purse. Each displayed her and her husband in various stages of nudity and in positions out of the ordinary. She refused to answer any of his questions but asked that the photos be returned. He stated that he considered them obscene and placed them in a sealed envelope pending another possible charge. Even with this threat, she refused to break her silence.

In contrast, Stuart seized the chance to cooperate and provided a two-page document outlining his involvement with his son and his son's activity with Art Williams. His confession ultimately proved problematic not only for Dale but also for Sergeant Hawkes. "Dad had no cause to feel uneasy," states Dale Elliott. "He asked me what to tell the cops and I told him to just tell them the truth. Dad's fear was something spurred on by the cops planting the seed in his mind."

On December 20, Hawkes' concern over the lack of evidence linking Williams to Elliott triggered a second visit to the Williams' property, this time in daylight. Kary, Malinowski, Thomas and Eppy made their way back over to Westdowne Road where they were met by Williams, Shirley Ferguson, Myron Zarry (the young mycologist working for Williams), and two young girls. They found nothing of significance until they reached the farthest corner of the property and came across the large structure referred to as the "barn." They had missed it on the 17th due to their "lack of familiarity with the property and the darkness of the early hours." Inside a small storage room about the size of a single-car garage, they found fifteen to twenty containers with labels indicating they held muriatic acid, sulphuric acid, aqua ammoniae, formic acid, benzene, methyl alcohol and hydrochloric acid, among other solutions. Kary seized six brown bottles, roughly one gallon in size, most of which were empty, though some contained a small amount of liquid. Sergeant Eppy once again documented the find with photographs after which they made their way back to the house.

They took Myron Zarry to the machine shop that he had rented next door. When Zarry climbed through a window, telling the police that Williams held the only key to the facility, the RCMP believed it confirmed their theory of a conspiracy involving Williams, Elliott and others jointly manufacturing and trafficking in contraband narcotics. For the cops that was the theory that held the most currency. In the shop, they found two empty twenty-five-pound containers, part of the shipment Williams had received from the CP Transport warehouse on August 24, 1972.

At the end of the day, Williams, Ferguson and Zarry were taken into custody and confined in the Duncan cells along with the Elliott family. It was only a matter of days before their individual bails were posted and could return home.

As investigations go, Williams' and Elliott's bust was a rare success, but by the time all the dust had settled, it would prove to be a partial victory at best.

Elliott's lab
Credit: Vancouver Appeals Court

Elliott's lab
Credit: Vancouver Appeals Court

RCMP evidence map of Elliott's lab
Credit: Vancouver Appeals Court

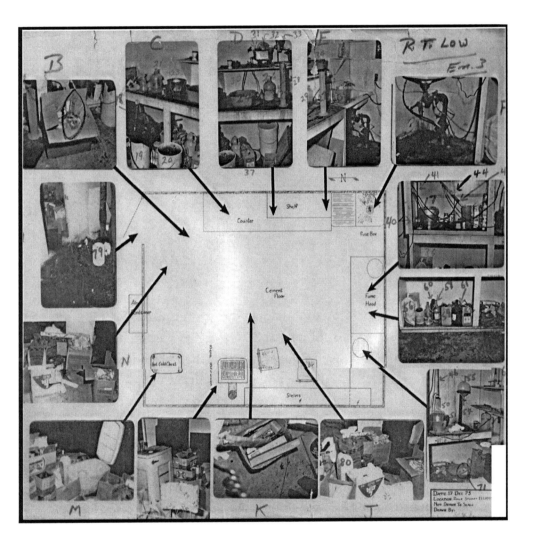

CHAPTER 10:

THE COURT IS IN SESSION

It was a hoot.

—Art Williams

On March 22, 1974, Art Williams, Shirley Ferguson, Dale Elliott, Jerry Elliott, the senior Elliotts and Myron Zarry stood before Judge J. Caldwell at the Duncan County Court as their preliminary hearing got underway. Allan Filmore represented all the accused. Sergeant Hawkes and chemist Don Saturley presented testimony on behalf of the prosecution, while the defense said nothing. At the close, Judge Caldwell found no cause for charges against Shirley Ferguson or Lois Elliott and granted them their freedom. Williams posted a $10,000 surety and agreed to report to the Ladysmith RCMP detachment daily. He also surrendered his passport, but the judge agreed he could regain it for the month of June so that he could complete an "important business trip" to Australia and New Zealand.

Spring and summer passed as Filmore prepared his clients' defense. On the world stage, the Viet Cong readied to attack Saigon. Patty Hearst had joined forces with her kidnappers, the Symbionese Liberation Army, with whom she cooperated in a bank hold-up and Richard Nixon refused to resign his presidency in the wake of Watergate.

The full cast for the MDA trial stood before Judge Leslie F. Cashman at the Nanaimo County Courthouse. After graduating from law school in 1949, Cashman had partnered with Don Currie and opened a practice in Quesnel, British Columbia. As is often the case in small Canadian towns, lawyers in a private practice who are respected by their peers, will be called on an ad hoc basis to act as Crown prosecutor where no permanent staffing is assigned. Respect for Cashman's fair and equitable approach to the law in this capacity led to his appointment to the bench on December 23, 1971. Three years later, he sat before Williams and his gang as his personal gavel lay on the block of the Nanaimo County Courthouse.

The lawyers who had represented Williams, Elliott and Zarry in the preliminary hearing in March had since been promoted to Crown Counsel in Nanaimo and Duncan. In Williams' and Elliott's view, given the personal information their lawyers knew about them, these promotions placed the lawyers in a conflict of interest should they ever have to face one another in a courtroom.

According to Elliott, Judge Cashman recognized the situation and quietly recommended to Williams, "Perhaps you would not go wrong if you spoke to someone from my old firm." As a result, Williams hired Henry Alan Hope, while Elliott employed Richard T. Low. "I wanted to go as far away from the local scene as possible to find a lawyer without going out of province," said Williams. "So, that's how I ended up hiring Alan."

Hope was a principal in the firm Hope, Heinrich & Hansen of Prince George, British Columbia. He was a fit and slender man of about five feet ten inches with a thick head of hair, and was held in high regard by his colleagues. Hope had sharpened his skills as a Crown prosecutor in Prince George, a community some seventy-three miles north of Cashman's former home of Quesnel. He was recognized for his success at prosecuting drug cases, and Williams felt confident the lawyer would be able to redirect that talent toward his defense.

"Hope drove down here and we made arrangements to pick up my files from my former lawyer's office," recounts Williams. "We picked up my stuff, put it in the back seat of Hope's Lincoln Continental and then locked it up in the Bastion parking lot in Nanaimo before driving out into the bush in my truck so we could rap. When we got back to the parking lot we saw this guy running away from Alan's car. I chased the guy down and grabbed him just as he was opening the door to his own car. I slammed him against the car and demanded to know what he was doing. He said he was a tax investigator for the City of Nanaimo and was just taking photos of the lot. When I got back to Alan's car, he said the guy had used a slim-gym on the passenger door and my files had been rifled."

Richard T. Low, Elliott's lawyer, was a "chunky thirty-year-old" with less than nine years of litigation under his belt. After graduating in 1964 from the University of British Columbia's law school, he articled in Victoria for a year and then headed off to Prince George to join the firm of F.A. Howard-Gibbon, Cashman, Hope, Heinrich, Hansen & Low. He had a passion for sports like hockey, skiing and golf, and he brought the same tenacity he displayed on the ice into the courtroom. As with most aggressive lawyers in small towns, Low was frequently called on to act as Crown prosecutor.

Hope and Low now faced the daunting task of working systematically through mountains of evidence, shredding as much as physically possible and casting doubt upon what remained. Williams and Elliott both knew that if they were convicted, it would be several years before they enjoyed freedom.

Under the provisions of the Food and Drugs Act and Amending Statutes, both Williams and Elliott were charged with conspiracy to traffic in MDA, trafficking in MDA and possession of MDA for trafficking.

From the first day until the closing remarks, Williams sat at the defense table scribbling a copious stream of observations. These notes would prove to be the foundation for tearing the Crown's evidence apart. The Crown prosecutors were Cecil O.D. Branson of the Victoria firm Jones, Emery and Carfa, and James D. Taylor of the Nanaimo firm Heath, Hutchinson. They called twenty-nine witnesses, including three chemists, the principal of which was Don Saturley, who gave evidence for the better part of ten days. As well, the Crown entered 227 exhibits and a few sub-exhibits. In contrast, the defense presented twelve exhibits and called no witnesses.

In short order, it became painfully clear that the prosecution had failed to secure sufficient evidence connecting Williams to the manufacture, possession or distribution of MDA. While Cec Branson did what he could to entwine Williams and, for that matter, Stuart Elliott, with Elliott and Zarry, Judge Cashman insisted that he was "not going to take the matter seriously unless Counsel had brought before him more than inference." In the judge's opinion, the paper containing a portion of the MDA formula written by Williams and retrieved from Dale Elliott's trailer was insufficient evidence to suggest the existence of a conspiracy. The nature of Williams' property was such that anyone could have wandered onto it, picked up the paper and deposited it in the trailer. The same principle applied to the lab equipment found in Elliott's keeping, which was clearly purchased and received by Williams. In Cashman's view, if Williams had wanted Elliott to have the formula for MDA, he would have seen that he received the entire formula for one or both stages of the process, not a segment of a single stage. Also, if the prosecution wanted to place such importance on that single piece of paper, how could it paint such a damming picture when it was recovered from an old apple box that was clearly "a receptacle for many diverse papers including three invoices from the House of Stein dated only a few days before the raid"?

An envelope was also found in the apple box with a handwritten recipe or experimentation on it to produce MDA. The postage date of April 27, 1972, followed the date when the manufacturing of MDA became illegal. Branson insisted that the handwriting of both Williams and Elliott be examined by an expert and compared against the evidence. As a result, three samples of the defendants' printing were made with their normal writing hand, and one sample with the other. When compared to the envelope, the expert was unable to find any similarities between the two.

When the RCMP raided the home of Myron Zarry and the Rieirson cabin, they found other pieces of paper with handwritten segments of either the first or second stage in the manufacturing of MDA. On the second floor of Zarry's home, in a baby's crib, they found a chart showing the natural sources of various drugs and a potency scale attached to each. They also found a list of chemicals labeled "hot chemicals," with no reference to their temperature. Words on the right-hand side of the paper indicated which were most watched and least watched. These papers were also handwritten, and again the prosecutors failed to establish whose penmanship was involved. Branson steered the RCMP chemist Don Saturley through each scrap of paper and attempted to show how together they made up the entire recipe. With the aid of Williams' notes, the defense could show how the quantities of chemicals shown on each paper differed from the other. This left Judge Cashman no choice but to dismiss the conspiracy theory altogether.

As Alan Hope and Richard Low cross-examined Saturley, they dissected his testimony and redirected his attention to the glass jars taken from each property. Each held a dark liquid in varying states of solidification. Low had the chemist correlate the formula written on each piece of paper to a specific jar. Saturley testified that the substance within each jar could be made into MDA crystals by carrying out one or more of the steps defined on the scraps of paper.

At this point, Low asked the court to allow him to take a 100-millilitre sample from each jar to the independent firm Econotech Services, in Vancouver, and have them prove or disprove Saturley's testimony. With Judge Cashman's consent, Low and Williams watched as Econotech chemists ran each sample through the steps defined on the individual pieces of paper. In each case the liquid failed to produce crystals.

When cross-examined, Saturley admitted that his own attempts to prove the liquids failed until he applied one method unfamiliar to the accused, which produced crystals. The defense argued that while he achieved his goal, he did so with a technique not known to Williams or Elliott, called "back extraction," and with equipment not found in their individual labs.

Saturley admitted to the court that he had never manufactured MDA so his knowledge on the subject was gained entirely from written material. The contents of another jar seized in Elliott's lab tested positive for ketone, but to the prosecution's misfortune, by the time it was brought forward as evidence the liquid had formed a solid mass at the bottom of the jar. Under cross-examination, Saturley said he was "at a loss" to explain the transition.

While winning one small battle may have bolstered Williams and Elliott's optimism, many others tipped to the prosecution's favor because of Saturley's testimony. By the end of the trial, his testimony would amount to 1,100 pages of transcript.

In hopes of showing a connection between Williams and Elliott, the Crown introduced the three Digi-scan radio receivers into evidence. One unit had been found in Elliott's trailer; another in the living quarters above his workshop. The last one was found in Williams' lab.

One of the receivers held crystals preset to the Victoria RCMP headquarters, the RCMP nationwide band, Victoria, Oak Bay and Saanich Police, who share the same frequency, the Attorney General's department in Victoria, the Vancouver City Detective Squad, and two additional channels for the Vancouver City Police. The remaining receivers were also connected to the stealth frequency secured by Vancouver Island's Criminal Investigations Unit. All receivers had a range of up to 100 miles.

Judge Cashman again felt led to reject the conspiracy theory when Jack Atkinson, a civilian radio technician employed by the RCMP examined the receivers and noted the crystals within the unit that Williams had were installed in a different order than those in Elliott's.

Cashman suggested that if the two parties had been working together, one would think they would have kept the crystals aligned to the same channels to avoid confusion in times of distress.

Hope cross-examined Bob Hawkes as to how thorough his search of Williams' and Elliott's property was and had he in fact seized all the crucial items from their buildings and land that were felt critical to the case. Hawkes confirmed that he had done a thorough job, to which Hope asked if he had seized the power cord for the scanners or their antenna and, furthermore, did he test each unit on site to insure they actually worked in their original setting. On all counts, he replied he had not. Hope responded that they were not operative devices used in the act of counter intelligence, but ornamental keepsakes taking up space.

Hope asked Hawkes how he managed to overlook the fifth scanner, which was in plain view when he returned to Williams' lab. Hawkes responded, "If I had seen it on the first visit, I would have seized it."

Evidence showed that during the six months preceding the December 17 raid, Williams and Elliott had contacted each other via their personal phone lines forty-five times. All but twelve calls were initiated from the phone located in the B.C. Institute of Mycology.

When Elliott's mother was taken to the Nanaimo RCMP Headquarters, her purse contained three wallets and a few letter-size envelopes, each of which contained a sizable amount of money. The currency had been neatly bundled in denominations ranging from $147 to $1,500. A black wallet bearing the initials "S.H.E.," corresponding to Dale's father, Stuart Hunter Elliott, held $2,900. Another black wallet identified by the initials "D.L.," held three bundles of $650 and two of $1,000. The third wallet also held a large sum of money but offered no identification. Also in her purse was a notebook with written amounts totaling $13,590.67.

At the time of her arrest she told Sergeant Colliar that the money was hers, yet when her husband stood in the witness box he testified his son had given the money to his mother. "Some of it he gave to her the day before the raid and the remainder sometime before that."

On the first day Dale's father made his way to the witness box, he was clearly intoxicated. When questioned, he was unresponsive and uncooperative, and when he was asked to look at a specific piece of evidence, his eyes remained locked in a glazed stupor. When questioned, he would not answer, but insisted upon asking questions of his own. The Crown labeled him as a reluctant witness and wanted him declared adverse or hostile.

During his second day of testimony he appeared more coherent, but his memory still managed to fail him on all matters except those considered basic or simple. For issues incriminating either of the accused, his memory completely escaped him. When shown his police statement and supporting testimony taken during the preliminary hearing, he either disagreed with the record, suggesting the words were given to him by Sergeant Hawkes or they were used as a means of escaping custody. When he did comply, and give evidence, he would request protection under the Canada Evidence Act. As it was, every now and then he would forget to request protection under the Act, leaving himself exposed to prosecution.

Elliott Sr. acknowledged that he "knew Williams, but had seldom seen him." He was aware that Williams was "building a large structure on his property and that his son Dale had worked for him in the erection of it," and that he once used the shed referred to as the Elliott lab, for woodworking.

When asked to repeat the written statement provided to the police, his memory failed him completely. In it he had written, "In the beginning Arthur was doing it all by himself, except for the selling which Dale handled. The way it stands right now, Art Williams makes the Ketone and Dale finishes it off. I did some of the capping for him but not all of it by a long way. I never knew what the stuff was but I should have known. I think at one time the woman living with Art, Shirley, did quite a bit of it. Dale's wife Ingrid used to cap for him too. We mixed it with Dextrose. Dale's sons Jerry and Raymond have been cooking it with Dale. I have never been involved in making it. Dale paid us three cents a cap and I think that they were selling it for $1.30 per cap which

Art and Dale split along with the expenses. The caps came from a Drug Store in Vancouver where he bought 100,000 of them. All the beakers and everything came through Art Williams. I saw him deliver the equipment. I didn't want to do this in the first place, but now I'm afraid of them and I really believe that one of them will shoot me if they find out I've talked. There is another guy Myron Zarry of Ladysmith, who used to make it too. On Friday, the wife and I capped 6,000 caps and put them in baggies of 100. A guy by the name of Roger Houston picked them up and Dale gave my wife $12,000 yesterday to keep for him."

Stuart Elliott wrote in his statement that he did some of the capping out of the sight of his wife during the late hours of the night and the early morning hours in a camper located on the property. He said he "put MDA crystals, which had a whitish color, onto a plate and mixed it with 70 percent dextrose, exactly as contained on a handwritten note and scooped a mixture of about 85 grams into the caps by holding each portion of the cap in either hand and pushing them together." The last time he did this would be about two months prior to December 17.

Stuart Elliott also told the court he had seen Williams on his son's property on several occasions but "could not remember precisely when." On one occasion, he saw Williams hand his son a brown jar. Crown Counsel presented Stuart Elliott with a number of brown jars and he identified one as being the same size, color and shape, but the cap was different. Saturley had testified that the jar in question had held Isosafrole, an insecticide that Williams applied to his mushroom beds, but Stuart Elliott stated that his son had told him that the jar contained Ketone. Since there was no evidence to support Stuart Elliott's statement, Judge Cashman stated he was "unable to place any reliance upon it."

Under cross-examination, Alan Hope, asked Stuart if he'd been promised immunity from prosecution if he gave the police the statement they wanted. When Stuart replied that he had been told that repeatedly, Judge Cashman stopped the proceedings to consider the circumstances in which the statement was taken, to determine whether or not the taking of the statement in itself was improper; if it had been given under any form of duress, or promise of hope, of advantage, or fear of prejudice.

After a brief discussion, the trial continued with prosecutor Branson calling Sergeant Hawkes to the stand to ask whether Stuart Elliott had been directed in the content of his statement. Hawkes testified that, "He [Stuart Elliott] started to cry, then he took his glasses off and started wiping his eyes. Constable Onischuk asked him if he was all right to which he said he was. And then he started saying that he knew he shouldn't have been involved in it. He seemed to be remorseful and that at first, he didn't know what was going on, but later he did. He stated that he was scared to get out because he had been beaten up before. He asked that I would not show the statement to anyone, which I agreed to. He stated that he feared for his life if someone was to find out he had given the statement. He figured someone would shoot him."

Under cross-examination Hope asked Hawkes if he had not gained Stuart Elliott's statement without reading him his rights and did he intend to use the statement as an investigative tool, as well as evidence against him? Hawkes replied, he had not read him his rights first and knew that rendered the document inadmissible as evidence against him." Did you intentionally mislead Stuart Elliott when you told him you would never show the statement to anybody or use it against him? "No." Did you not say while giving evidence during this hearing that he was concerned about anybody seeing it and that you would not show it to anybody? "Yes." Regardless of the promise, the statement was made public and presented as evidence within this trial.

After spending the better part of a week in the witness box, Stuart Elliott was called morally bankrupt by the prosecution. Even the judge suggested that he felt Stuart "knew a great deal more than he was letting on" and was "not a credible witness." Cashman considered the testimony worthless and removed it as evidence saying: "His [Stuart Elliott's] defense, that he had a poor memory, was his only fortress against issues that clearly threatened his freedom, when on other occasions he was willing to say anything to please his questioner and advance his own position."

Dale Elliott later commented on his father's testimony, "I didn't care what he said. They got me fair and square. They just got my dad talking and when he realized what he was saying he relied on his absent-mindedness to defray the damage."

Each day at the close of the trial, Williams would return home and re-enact the events that unfolded to those around him. According to Happy Laffin, "He would run around his living room like a lunatic and act out the part of each character from a different corner of the room. He would turn his hat a different way and imitate the judge, then scamper over to another corner and impersonate the prosecutor. It was a real hoot."

Dale Elliott with his parents
Credit: Dale Elliott

Judge Leslie Cashman
Credit: Leslie Cashman

Elliott's children
Monica, Raymond
& Steve
Credit: Dale Elliott

CHAPTER 11:

JUDGMENT DAY

In my view, the cumulative effect of the evidence directly admissible against Williams is as consistent with that of Elliott working alone.

—Judge Leslie F. Cashman

Judge Cashman presented his findings on January 21, 1975, in the form of an eighty-two-page judgment. He wasted no time in dismissing Dale's son, Jerry Dean Elliott, even though he was caught exiting the lab during the raid. He was less enthusiastic about dismissing Elliott's parents because there was some evidence that one or both might have been co-conspirators. Cashman also dismissed Shirley Ferguson without much ado.

As for Myron Zarry, Crown Counsel could demonstrate that there was sufficient evidence to draw an inference that Zarry may well have been a party with Elliott in a scheme to manufacture MDA. In their words, "Myron Zarry had all the chemical expertise needed to assist Elliott." Yet, the judge found him not guilty of any of the charges, stating, "The evidence was insufficient to find him a party to any agreement."

Throughout the trial, the defense lawyers, with the exception of Dale Elliott's, suggested that Elliott was the only party who "had all the equipment and knowledge to perform the various stages necessary to produce MDA including the production of ketone."

The Crown was adamant that Dale Elliott and Arthur Williams had conspired to traffic in MDA and that it had been produced by a chemical formula or recipe, involving a two-stage process, the author of which was Arthur Williams. At trial, the Crown argued that, "Stage 1 involves the production of a substance called ketone, the starting material which was made by Williams in one place and received by Elliott who followed the steps in stage 2, converting ketone to MDA. It was then packaged and sold. It claimed Williams was the brains of the operation and was the only one who possessed the background and training to synthesize the formula. It claimed the formula is the one contained in the typewritten piece of paper taken from the hands of Williams on December 17, 1973." Yet, it was Cashman's opinion that "the vast majority of evidence placed before the Court was subjective, inconclusive and at its best, rested upon inference."

During the trial, the Crown presented evidence that inferred Williams had conducted experiments not only with MDA but also with other restricted hallucinogenic drugs. They relied on a letter addressed to Arthur James Williams from Tord E. Svenson, dated September 20, 1967, which dealt with the experimentation of LSD. They suggested the letter showed Williams as having a "general interest towards hallucinogenic substances." Cashman dismissed the letter, saying "It is clear the letter invited further inquiry but none appears to have been forthcoming."

Under cross-examination by Williams' lawyer, Don Saturley indicated that, if Williams was the person who conducted the experiments in the production of MDA, he was mainly concerned with quality and yield. To this, Judge Les Cashman wrote, "With respect to the concern for quality and yield on the part of the experimenter, it is more consistent with a legal manufacture of MDA for legitimate purposes rather than for illicit purposes."

Although a significant amount of court time had been consumed on Saturley, Judge Cashman summed up the value of his testimony as: "Prior to this time he had participated in two raids of clandestine laboratories engaged in the manufacture of MDA. He has had no experience in the manufacture of any drug . . . and that fact renders his opinion theoretical." In short, Cashman disqualified Saturley as an expert.

Cashman held that when it came to Williams, "it is not an offence to have an interest in such matters so long as one does not do any of the things specified in the Act"; he therefore found no evidence linking Williams with Elliott in the manufacturing or trafficking of MDA. "Nor can Counsel demonstrate that conspiracy existed between Williams and Elliott. The crime of conspiracy is committed the moment two or more have agreed that they will do, at once or at some future time, certain things."

Cashman noted, "There was undoubtedly an association between Elliott and Williams . . . as found in the phone calls, the joint purchase of the Elliott property, the evidence of certain bills and receipts pertaining to Elliott which were found in Williams' possession, amongst other unsubstantiated statements made by Stuart Elliott and the fact that equipment purchased by Williams through the B.C. Institute of Mycology found its way onto Elliott's property. There was the patent for a cap-making machine that was found among Williams' files. There can be no doubt that Williams had a background and the facilities to produce MDA, and I am satisfied I can draw an inference that he did experiment with and produce MDA along with other hallucinogenic drugs. However, as Saturley testified, ten chemicals were needed to produce MDA, and four of those, namely: hydrogen peroxide, formic acid, acetone and magnesium sulphate, were not found in Williams' lab. At the time of the raid there was no lingering MDA residue in the lab or the pungent odor that was near impossible to fully eradicate from a room. The police stated that they had conducted a thorough search of Williams' entire property, which included a large structure under construction at the rear of his land, with them finding no further evidence."

Judge Cashman concluded, "In my view, the cumulative effect of the evidence directly admissible against Williams is as consistent with that of Elliott working alone. The evidence is also consistent with Elliott working with Zarry to produce MDA. That being so, I am compelled to find that the Crown has failed to prove an agreement between Elliott and Williams and has likewise failed to prove an agreement between Elliott and any other person. In the result, I find Dale Elliott and Arthur Williams not guilty of conspiracy to traffic in MDA."

During the trial, the evidence presented showed that "669,832 milligrams of MDA Hydrochloride (salt of MDA) had been found in Elliot's lab, and if mixed with a quantity of dextrose or lactose, it would produce 11,163 #4 caps such as one would expect to find offered on the illicit market." Corroborated by his father's testimony, it was clear Dale Elliott had been manufacturing MDA for some time, and with the police finding 36,000 #4 caps, the fact that Elliott was involved in the drug trade was hard to dispute.

Crown Counsel Branson submitted that Williams had aided and abetted Elliott in the production of MDA by (1) supplying him with information on its manufacture, (2) supplying him with chemical equipment, or (3) supplying him with Ketone.

Cashman's response was, "I am not satisfied beyond a reasonable doubt that Williams did any one or more of the three things which the Crown relies upon for a conviction. There are other rational explanations for the supply of equipment diverted from BC Institute of Mycology to Elliott. There are as well rational explanations for Elliott's source of knowledge."

Cashman found Williams not guilty of trafficking, a verdict that did not sit well with the prosecution. He concluded that, "the court is entitled to draw an inference from the large quantity of MDA, #4 caps and the extensive equipment for making MDA found in the Elliott lab, as well as the evidence of Sergeant O'Neill and Stuart Elliott, that Dale Elliott did not have MDA solely for his own use." He therefore found Dale Stuart Elliott and only him, guilty of trafficking in MDA.

Dale Elliott was convicted and on February 24, 1975 received the maximum allowable sentence of ten years. He was led off straight away to the Matsqui Penitentiary in Abbotsford. Art Williams, on the other hand, was a free man. Before long, word on the street said that he was again open for business, brazened following his victory and sure he could outwit the legal system once again if needed.

At the close of the trial Don Bohun submitted an appeal and request for Dale Elliott's release on bail. On March 20, 1975, bail was denied, to which Bohun submitted a second request which succeeded on October 14. At the second bail hearing the prosecution declared Elliott a threat to society, claiming that if he were released, he would "likely return to his production of MDA." Bohun argued that the RCMP had given testimony during the trial that if Elliott were released, he would be unable to produce MDA since they had seized all his equipment and his stash of chemicals. Bohun added that it was next to impossible for Elliott to help him prepare an appeal to his conviction while incarcerated. He stated, "The only phone available to Elliott was in a public area of the jail where calls were limited to three minutes while being monitored and recorded. Forcing me to travel to and from Vancouver each time I need my client's input is unreasonable."

The appeal against Elliott's conviction was taken up by Richard Low, who claimed an injustice had occurred against his client when Don Saturley tested the various liquids seized as evidence without the presence of the defense, thereby robbing the defense of its ability to cross-examine his analytical technique. "Those tests should have been conducted by an independent consultant."

The primary grounds for Low's application came from Saturley's testimony, where he stated that MDA and the Hydrochloride Salt of MDA were the same drug. Richard Low stated that, although the Crown has been speaking of a drug that had the same base, the two were in fact quite different from each other. Because the charges made no reference to a "Salt of MDA," there were no grounds upon which his client could face a conviction.

The Court of Appeal accepted Low's argument and overturned Elliott's earlier conviction. Dale Elliott was once again a free man, though the Crown immediately commenced work to change that.

During the trial, the Crown had asked the court to stay the third count against Williams and Elliott, that of possession of MDA for the purpose of trafficking. None of the defense lawyers had recognized the downside at the time, but the Crown set about to appeal Elliott's acquittal, rewriting count three in hopes of sealing up the cracks through which the original case had slid. The new application would redefine the substance which was found in Elliott's keeping as being a salt of MDA.

Bohun once again stepped up to defend Elliott, but not until he had been guaranteed financial support from the Legal Aid Society. "Dale Elliott didn't have the funds needed to fight his case to a higher level. While the case was very narrow and required only a few pages of transcript to address the motion, prosecutors Branson and Taylor demanded that Bohun provide twenty copies of his entire trial transcript and deliver them to the Supreme Court Justices in Ottawa prior to the hearing." According to Bohun, "Copy and freight alone cost me just shy of $10,000. Dale had to rent a U-Haul to transport all the material and by the time he had finished loading, the truck was full. Elliott drove the U-Haul to Calgary where he would fly the rest of the way to Ottawa.

While Elliott was in Calgary, he decided to do a bit of business. One of the problems he and Williams faced was the constant need for formic acid, an integral part of manufacturing MDA. If they delayed in getting their hands on it, production came to a grinding halt, and that simply wasn't good for business. When Elliott left Vancouver on route to Ottawa, he called MacKenzie & Feimann Ltd. in Calgary and presented himself as Don Henderson of Barney Creek Mines in Mission, BC. Art had dealings with the MacKenzie & Feimann's Vancouver office, but he and Elliott figured the judicial heat made it prudent to go further afield with a fresh identity. The company's receiver said they had what they needed, so Elliott told them a guy who was backhauling from out east would pick up the load but he would only be carrying cash.

"Unfortunately, I got waylaid in Ottawa so I called them again to alter my imaginary driver's date of arrival. I told them his father had passed away. They were tactful enough not to question me further. On my return trip, I stopped over at Calgary and phoned them again, changing my voice to a heavy English accent while assuming the character of my imaginary driver. I told them the heater core had gone on my truck and asked if someone could help me load the five-gallon pails into a stretched Budget rental van. No problem!

By the time, we were finished loading the van, it was filled from front to back and right to the ceiling. Rather than drive it all the way home, I took it over to the CP Freight office and shipped it attention Barney Creek Mines of Mission, BC. This was a fictitious company, so I asked the freight company to hold it in their warehouse and someone would pick it up. We got rid of the van, flew back to Vancouver and then on to Victoria. I drove back over to the mainland during the following week and picked up the shipment without incident."

The principle of full disclosure demands that the prosecution disclose all information pertinent to the defense's case, whether it helps their cause or not. Bohun felt that Branson and Taylor were determined to thwart his efforts. In the end, the tit-for-tat battle did nothing to promote Elliott's cause. "When our application for Legal Aid was non-responsive, out of sheer desperation, Bohun started the MDA Defense Fund and promoted it by distributing flyers all over the regional area." By the time the appeal trial arrived, they had raised all that they needed.

On November 26, 1975, Judges Bull, Branca and Taggart of the Supreme Court of Canada rendered a verdict that the grounds upon which the Crown had appealed Elliott's acquittal were insufficient to overturn the lower court's decision. Furthermore, they ruled the Crown could not alter the third count after the fact to reflect a 'Salt of MDA,' as it placed the defendant at an unfair disadvantage. The Supreme Court stated that the lower court had exceeded its powers in allowing the amendment to the third charge and thereby ordering a new trial.

The Crown's appeal failed, and Elliott's acquittal was upheld.

During the trial and Dale Elliott's wait for bail, both his and Art's troubles were not limited to those brought on by the RCMP. Back on August 16, 1974, Revenue Canada had laid claim to a portion of their personal earnings and that of the BC Institute of Mycology. Per a Federal Court of Canada affidavit, Williams and his Institute of Mycology owed $64,523.56 plus interest in unpaid taxes. He had hoped to use the Society as a shelter to evade taxes, but this only proved to be his downfall. The feds claimed that the equipment purchased by The BC Institute of Mycology was in fact used for the illegal production of MDA and rendered any guarantee of tax exemptions null and void.

With writ in hand, Alfred Savage and his team from Revenue Canada swept through Elliott's home and property, collecting every scrap of paper that could help prove their case, finally concluding that he also owed $62,625.29 plus interest. At the same time, an official from the sheriff's office arrived and seized his hand tools, lathes, power tools, motorcycles, personal vehicle and his impressive gun collection, plus any money that Ingrid had in her purse. Dale states, "They even tried to remove Ingrid's wedding ring but stopped when it became apparent she would suffer physical injury before giving it up". Not stopping there, they garnisheed the balance of Elliott's bank account. Doman's Transport was commissioned to load everything and take it to Quarterway Auction Sales in Duncan. Following the seizure, the RCMP appeared with BC Hydro and disconnected the power, depriving Ingrid and her children of heat, water and the ability to cook, even though their hydro account was paid in full. Before Elliott could get an injunction, all his worldly possessions were auctioned to the highest bidder for a meager $10,763.50.

CHAPTER 12:

HARD TO FIND

*We got to the point where we could tear down a lab and clean
everything up in twenty minutes.*

—Lou Brown

In the fall of 1976, the RCMP noticed that Williams and Elliott had
taken an interest in off-road dirt bikes. On a few occasions the RCMP
had witnessed both parties scooting off into the forest that backed onto
Williams' land and then along the power-line right-of-way that ran
parallel to the highway. Thinking they may be onto something, the
RCMP searched the right-of-way with tracking dogs but found nothing.

Dale Elliott recalls, "We were looking for a lab site that gave us an
advantage over anyone who came into the area. High up on the south
face of Mount Brenton, located five miles south of Ladysmith, I found
this old deck of logs that had been fallen and abandoned sometime in
the 1930s. They were covered in thick moss and dirt. I took my twelve-
inch McCullough chainsaw and cut out a doorway in the side and down
through the logs until I had a room six feet by fifteen feet and high enough
to stand up in. From there I went up the creek, which was just off a way

and felled a couple trees to dam it up. I laid down a plastic liner to trap the water and buried a three-quarter-inch plastic hose all the way back down the mountain to the cave. It gave us clean water year-round at eighty pounds of pressure.

Lou Brown built the cabin about 200 feet uphill from the cave, and Dale Elliott diverted a water line to it. From the cabin, they could see all the way down to the intersection of River Road and the Trans-Canada Highway, so if anyone drove into the area, they would monitor the dust trail to determine if they were going to have an uninvited visitor or not. Brown stated, "When the gang started seeing a few too many footprints around the area, we set up a couple of cameras so we could see if anything was happening outside the lab. The last thing we wanted was to pop our heads up right into the laps of the cops. We got to the point where we could tear down a lab and clean everything up in twenty minutes."

There were three ways the men could reach the cabin. One was along an old skid road to a point above the cabin, from which they could make their way a couple hundred yards down through the trees. Another route was via the power line that ran from behind Art's place. They carved out a trail from there up the steep slope to the cabin. It was quite a haul so when they travelled that route they carried next to nothing on their backs. One additional route was only used if a quick exit was needed. With this route, the men would go straight downhill from the cabin to a high ledge that had a swampy area beneath it, then jump out and grab one of the longer branches of an old cedar that grew alongside the precipice, then swing out like Tarzan, dropping to the dry land on the far side of the bog. The guys would get bruised up pretty good with this method but the physical damage was no worse than what a pair of police restraints would cause.

In each case the dirt bikes were used to get within hiking distance of the lab. On the bikes, they could make it from Art's place to the mountain lab in three-quarters of an hour, which was the fastest means to get there. When they had ridden as far as they could, they would haul the generator and the propane cylinders the remaining distance to the lab, strapped to an old Trapper Nelson backpack. The generator could run the flash evaporator and a couple of lights for about four hours on a tank of gas. It ran so quiet it was impossible to hear it unless someone was standing right beside it.

By January 1977, the volume of MDA on the streets had reached an all-time high forcing the RCMP to kick their surveillance back into high gear. Back on December 30, 1976, a subordinate to Bob Hawkes, Corporal Chester Kary had followed a tip from a hiker who had been accosted by a couple of youths riding dirt bikes as the hiker picked his way across the south face of Mount Brenton. The youths on bikes had told the hiker they didn't want to see him ever again on that side of the mountain.

Before the hiker could pick his way back down to River Road, which served the area, he ran into Williams, who was on his way up the mountain. Williams also lashed out at the hiker and told him he was trespassing. The hiker knew of Art vaguely but decided it would be best if he never let on. The RCMP were mystified by the report, but with further investigation discovered that Arthur Williams held a miner's license on the mountain.

About the same time, Kary also received a report from a forestry worker who had made a mental note of questionable characters coming and going in the same area. The RCMP became convinced that Williams was operating an MDA lab somewhere on the mountain. Kary recalls, "We didn't want to raise suspicion, so we made several attempts to comb the mountain dressed as hikers, then another time as forestry workers and yet another attired as hunters. We tried approaching the site from every direction, but because of a bluff and the steep terrain, we had no alternative but to use the route reported by the hiker."

Twenty paces off the road, anyone walking in the area became totally disoriented unless they stuck to the trail that Williams and his boys had beaten down. To the sides and underfoot was nothing more than a leg breaking tangle of roots and branches. Every fifty feet or so, a moss-covered wall of fallen trees, taller than the average man and a hundred feet long, forced them to alter their course. These walls served as a breeding ground for young saplings that had found nourishment in the decaying bark.

The RCMP took to using bikes themselves. According to Elliot, "On one occasion we were riding up River Road and the cops started following us on bikes. Art was wearing a black helmet with a tinted visor so you couldn't see his face. When they caught up to us, I made an abrupt right turn straight into the trees and just kept going. One of the cops tried to follow me, but after taking a few too many branches across his face he abandoned the pursuit. The other guy kept following Art, all the time trying to get him to stop by waving his badge. At a convenient spot, Art slowed down long enough to let the fellow pull up along his left side. At a point in the road where the edge dropped straight down into the Koksilah River, Art fell back just enough to boot the guy's handlebars hard over to the left. As expected the cop lost control and went careening down into the river. A few weeks later we were all in court for something, I don't remember what and this guy walks in with a partial body cast and one arm suspended over his head. He was a pitiful sight."

The cops were so concerned about running into Williams, Elliott or any of his inner circle, that progress was severely hampered for the better part of two months. Kary even resorted to studying aerial photos in hopes the lab would stand out against the mountain foliage, but they were of little use.

It was only through a stroke of luck they found the lab. One day a couple of Kary's men became disoriented high up on the southeast side of the mountain and stumbled upon an eight-by-ten-foot log cabin hidden at the toe of a rock bluff and behind a dense clump of trees. Draped across the roof was camouflage netting. Kary recalls, "It was a long way up the mountain. The interior was sparsely furnished, with a small table, a couple of benches, a stove and some provisions from which meals could be prepared. There was no sign of a chemical lab, but I was confident I would find a lab close by." It was just a matter of time until his suspicion proved valid.

On one occasion when Kary and a couple of his men were making their way to the site, they heard a motorcycle making its way down the mountain toward them. With barely enough time to dive into the nearby bush, they watched two men approach on a red dirt bike. Kary identified the driver as Dale Elliott, while the male passenger with long blond hair passed without being recognized. After the bike had left the area, they brushed themselves off and continued making their way up the mountain.

Following a strenuous hike, the police found the cabin locked up tight. Everyone fanned out, searching for clues that might connect the cabin to Elliott, Williams or one of their inner circles. As they approached the area, they were struck by a strong odor of gasoline. Beside the trail, they found a second Honda motorcycle, similar to the one that had passed them earlier, and jerry cans full of fuel.

There was also a cache of plastic five-gallon containers buried just off the path to the cabin, covered by bark and leaves and a few propane cylinders on a bench of land beside a stream some 250 feet east of the cabin. Hidden in a dugout immediately in front of the cabin was a 300-watt Honda generator connected to electrical cables that ran off in several directions.

While Williams never fully comprehended the magnitude of the resources arrayed against him, the RCMP was equally unable to grasp the ingenuity of Arthur Williams. It was his nature to trade certainty for possibility each time he matched wits with his adversary, and over the years, many of the RCMP have come to acknowledge and in an odd way respect his brilliance. They knew, for instance, that Williams and Elliott would be on guard; what they didn't know was that one of Williams' friends had managed to break into the RCMP offices after hours and had a thorough read of the Arthur Williams file. The fellow stated, "As a volunteer fireman, we would party in the basement of the RCMP offices because the fire hall had no suitable room. I could hold my liquor pretty good, but on the night in question the cops that partied with us were all hammered. I just waited until the last one nodded off, then I walked upstairs and searched through their file cabinets until I found Art's file. It made for dry reading but nonetheless Art found the contents confirmed some of his suspicions as to who was watching him and when, those bugs that had already been planted and the fact that there was a traitor in his midst, identified only as a number."

Corporal Chester Kary, a subordinate to Bob Hawkes, eventually took over the investigation and in short order received authorization to place wiretaps on phones belonging to Williams, Elliott and many of their associates. However, it wasn't long before the RCMP realized that no matter how hard they worked, they could never come close to locking them up. One big problem was that they had no chance of discovering firsthand what kind of organization Williams was running. Their only hope was to uncover and control someone already near the center, someone who could strike at the heart of the organization and set it off balance from the inside out. They started to look for a soft spot within Williams' hierarchy, for a man who would collapse under pressure, a man reluctant to go to jail to protect his friends, but the RCMP discovered that Williams' associates were loyal to a fault.

Williams began showing signs of paranoia. As Lou Brown recalls, "Every now and then pretty girls would show up at Art's place asking for drugs. Art would ask them what they had been busted for. When confronted Art's comment would shake them up so much that they would turn and leave empty-handed. The cops were arresting them for possession or the likes and then let them walk if they agreed to try and entrap Art." While Williams was becoming paranoid, he was also becoming bolder in his countermeasures. He would lie awake at night dreaming up cat-and-mouse schemes to thwart or distract the police. If it was a game the authorities wanted to play, he was going to make it as interesting as possible. Williams truly believed the RCMP were no match for his cunning and this proved to be his greatest miscalculation.

During the first week of February 1977, Kary learned that Williams would be out of town for a week while Elliott was scheduled to be in Ottawa to attend a Supreme Court proceeding dealing with the Crown's appeal for a new trial on his 1973 possession charge. The cops would never have a better opening, so on February 8, Kary, in the company of a dog handler and nine other officers, made yet another trek up the mountain just to observe.

The dog made a beeline for a stash of chemicals buried near the cabin, but after several hours with no further success, they grew weary. Kary said, "We had swept the entire area around the cabin to a point roughly 200 feet above it and below the top of the bluff. We had spent hours at it to the point where we were all bagged and all we wanted to do was go home. Several of my men plunked themselves down on a pile of logs which were situated about seventy feet below where we had found the propane cylinders and proceeded to give their feet a needed rest as they lit up a smoke. Somewhat ticked and out of sheer frustration from our lack of success, I wandered over to the fellows and asked them what they were doing. Waiting for an obvious answer, I flicked a broken branch I had been holding towards the leaves and debris spread across the ground at the base of the logs my guys were sitting on. To my surprise, the branch scraped against something hard and I noticed a glint of tin shining beneath the leaves that ran inward under the logs. At the same moment one of the guys piped up and commented that there was no way on earth they were going to find the lab, to which I responded, 'Did you think of looking under the logs you're sitting on?'

"Sometimes police work is just like that. If you turn over enough rocks during any investigation, sooner or later you will find what you are looking for. So, I brushed the leaves off and there was this sheet of tin. When I pulled it back and shone my flashlight in, I could see into this narrow shaft that had been cut out of the four-foot-diameter logs. The shaft led into a cave that had been dug out of the dirt. Directly below the entrance I could see a bench with a two-burner stove on it, plus a bunch of other apparatus, and there was a tray of liquid sitting over the burner. I thought it was best not to disturb the setting so we called it a day."

On February 10, Kary returned to the mountain, this time with two toxicologists from the Crime Detection Department, and an expert locksmith to help him gain access to the cabin. As they approached the area, they could hear the generator running. No one appeared to be around, but a piece of timber was propped against the door of the cabin to hold it closed.

Inside they found a quantity of food in plastic containers, a loft with a foam mattress, and one of the fellows pulled a .308 rifle from where it was stashed up between the ceiling rafters. There was a wooden box that held copies of the Western Producer and the Chemainus Daily Observer, one of which bore an address label with Arthur Williams' name on it. The evidence was starting to mount.

Kary made his way down the eroded creek bed, ducking and scaling fallen trees, until he was close to the cave. There he could hear two male voices, the clanging of containers and various utensils. He could just make out the entrance to the cave through the trees when out popped one of Williams' soldiers, whom Kary identified as Ray Ridge. Hoping to protect his cover, Kary moved off to a safe distance and monitored the two with binoculars until they had left the mountain. With daylight fading, Kary and his crew also left the area.

On February 14, Kary returned once again with a couple of his men. The access he had uncovered on his first visit didn't seem feasible as the sole means of coming and going, because it dropped directly onto the workbench and burner. It seemed more appropriate as a source of fresh air, so he continued to probe the outside of the pile of logs, trying not to disturb the overgrowth. In time, one of his men noticed a large, thick piece of bark lying halfway down the log pile. When it was moved, it exposed what Kary had been looking for. The access was somewhat larger than the prior opening and veered off at a 90-degree angle into the interior. It required some agility to squeeze through and then navigate the route, but once inside the officers found themselves in a spacious area with plenty of headroom. On the left, a one-inch-diameter plastic pipe led to a faucet and a large metal pot that served as a washbasin. There was also an electrical conduit coming from a small breaker box and feeding a single light bulb. One of his men headed back outside and followed the plastic pipe from the outside wall of the lab, where it was skillfully buried under a layer of moss. The pipe wove its way up the mountain a few hundred yards to where it surfaced in a pile of rocks carefully arranged in the center of a small creek to create a catchment area. In turn, the electrical conduit led up the mountain to the Honda generator near the cabin.

Back inside the lab there was a container filled with liquid sitting on the table beside the two-burner stove, a condensing apparatus and a Variac, AC transformer. With enough information to fill a notebook, Kary and his crew left the area, making certain everything was as they had found it.

Knowing physical surveillance would eventually be compromised by the single route into the area, Kary decided to get their bugging experts, John Deering and Willing Mino to conceal a radio-activated bug in the roof of the cave so they could turn it on and off, allowing the battery to last that much longer. They were confident it would transmit all the way to Duncan because of the elevation.

It would take two trips, the first of which was to carry in a roll of wire and all the other electronic paraphernalia they needed. The second trip would allow them time to bury the wire from the battery up the hill to the transmitter in the cave. The first leg of the work went off without a hitch so the second trip was scheduled for February 18th.

It didn't take long on the 18th for Kary and his boys to realize that something had gone terribly wrong. While they had used every means possible to hide their supplies, when they returned they discovered that their cache was no longer there. Kary made his way up to the cave and was shocked to discover a gaping hole where it once sat. The smell of dynamite still hung in the air from the explosion that had scattered the massive logs like toothpicks and left the area strewn with equipment. The RCMP figured that they must have tripped a non-explosive detonator that Williams, whom they knew had counter-intelligence and explosives experience from the war, had rigged on the mountain. In fact, it was Williams and Ray Ridge who had blown up the lab with a half case of dynamite. It was apparent to them that someone had discovered the site based on the amount of litter carelessly thrown onto the ground. As Dale Elliott explains, "We knew when we started to have visitors up on the mountain because we always took extra precaution and cleaned up after ourselves, taking our garbage out with us. Unlike the cops, we never discarded gum wrappers on the ground and we knew the imprint of the boots we wore, so when different ones started showing up in the mud, we figured it was time to relocate. After the cops had been up there with their equipment, there were so many fresh prints in the dirt and moss that we just followed their tracks until we found their stash. Blowing that lab was a simple business calculation. We had a few others running elsewhere so it didn't interrupt us."

It was not until Kary's final visit on June 3rd that he decided to collect some of the evidence that was scattered about the area. With the lab in ruins, the police felt thwarted once again. A few months later as Kary searched Williams' home, he came across a crudely drawn map that showed the location where Kary's men had hid their supplies. He also found a photograph of Elliott and another man standing over the remains of the cave, smiling and holding a newspaper that had the words "F_ _ _ the Pigs" scrawled across it with a black pen. Ever since his early years, Art had exhibited a preference for playing it close to the edge, sometimes literally.

Aerial showing Williams home, power line & Mt. Brenton lab
Credit: Google Earth

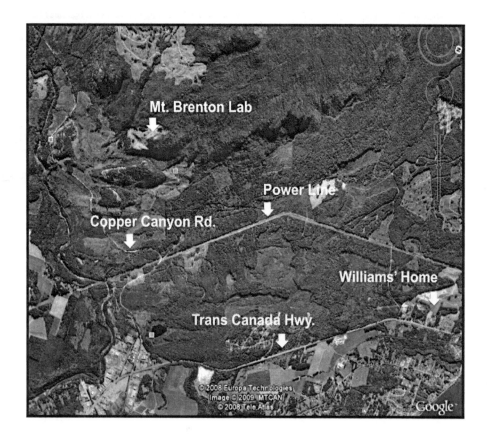

Elliott at Mt. Brenton cabin
Credit: Daryl Ashby

Mt. Brenton cave lab
Credit: Vancouver Appeals Court

Interior Mt. Brenton cabin 2008
Credit: Daryl Ashby

CHAPTER 13:

BUSINESS IN BELIZE

Art had an appointment with the mayor of Belize … to investigate
business opportunities.

—Shirley Ferguson

In September 1976, Williams formed a new company that would act as a holding company for an aircraft and provide him with another avenue of tax relief. Williams assumed the role of president, while Paul Jackson, his flying instructor from Victoria, was secretary. There were two other directors, his friend and lawyer Don Bohun of Ladysmith and Maurice Peter Tanchak of Coquitlam, B.C., whom Williams had known from his archery days. Williams named the company Inkster Aircraft Corporation. When Paul Jackson asked him why he'd come up with the name Inkster Air, he [Art] had replied, 'I just wanted to irk a young up-and-comer in the RCMP named Norman Inkster.'" (Inkster quickly rose through the ranks to become the chief commissioner of the RCMP and then the head of Interpol. Following his retirement, he partnered as CEO of one of the world's most powerful investigative think tanks.)

On March 25, 1977, Williams traded a fist-full of crisp bills for a brand new, single-engine, four-seat Cessna 172 Hawk XP aircraft. Williams stated, "The XP stood for extra power." Purchased from J.R. Harrison Aircraft in Sidney, B.C., his new set of wings could carry a payload up to 985.5 pounds.

June Harrison and her husband were the owners of Harrison Air and she recalls the purchase as if it were yesterday. "Art paid cash for IWQ and Bob [her husband] didn't know what to do with the money as the bank would likely question its source, but I told him to just deposit it and we would deal with the bank if necessary."

In total, two planes were acquired, a Cessna 150, which Williams used for short hops, and the Cessna 172 Skyhawk, which he employed for longer excursions. Wishing to diversify his holdings, he and Jackson opened a flight school at the Nanaimo Airport. Williams also joined forces with Stanley Cross and Stanley's cousin Ralph Harris to purchase all the components needed to assemble two small helicopters, but nothing ever came of the last two ventures.

To escape prying eyes, Williams took regular joy rides over the Strait of Georgia towards the mainland or up into the area of Desolation Sound, a very isolated wilderness area, just to soothe his rattled nerves. As time progressed he found cause to increase the number of flights associated with his ever-expanding business. Some jaunts took him south of the border, well beyond the boundaries of what a novice flier would consider comfortable. Seldom would he take the time to check in with the US Customs if it appeared inconvenient or risky to do. On those occasions, he would switch off his transponder and then slip in and out at a low altitude beneath their radar.

Paul Jackson's son Richard described Williams as an "indifferent flier, because he had an inflated opinion of himself. He wasn't a particularly good pilot in my opinion. He insisted on flying in bad weather all the time. He just liked to get places and didn't like to be held up by anything. If he was going somewhere, he had to do it now and not at a time convenient to others."

Williams flew almost daily. In November 1977, he reported to Transport Canada that he had logged 1,500 hours that year, more than most commercial pilot's log. And for weeks on end the police would go to the Cassidy Airport to watch him come and go. They had no idea where he was going or why, because he wasn't the kind of pilot who would file a flight plan. It was a foolproof system. Williams could use his plane to rendezvous with his associates at an isolated field where he would pick up his raw materials or deliver the product he had finished before returning home. If he thought he was going to have some uninvited company at his landing site, he would make a mental note as to where he was, drop the package out the window of the plane and have someone retrieve it later.

A Cassidy Airport radio operator suggested Williams had made numerous trips south of the border, stopping at Friday Harbor on San Juan Island if it suited him to clear customs. The RCMP contacted US Customs but could locate records for only two trips into the US.

On April 4, 1977, Williams flew his 172 Cessna out of the Cassidy Airport, located six miles south of Nanaimo, in the company of Don Bohun on what Bohun referred to as a "business trip." "Art had an appointment with the mayor of Belize," states Shirley Ferguson. "He wanted to investigate business opportunities there."

The sky above Cassidy was clear as their Cessna left the tarmac with no wind and thirty-two kilometers of visibility. The coastline however was socked in with fog, but by the time they had covered the first forty miles, they were high enough to see over the coastal blemish.

At the end of the first day, the two had cleared US Customs and settled for the night in Boise, Idaho. After refueling, they picked their way across the US in a southeasterly direction, touching down for the second night and more fuel in Wichita, Kansas. The routine continued until the third night in St. Petersburg, Florida. From St. Petersburg, Williams had calculated they would fly to Key West where they'd top up their tanks, then continue 360 miles due south across the open body of water known as the Straits of Florida. This would place them along the edge of the notorious Bermuda Triangle after which they would pass over the island of Cuba before touching down in George Town,

Grand Cayman Islands. From there he envisioned a dead-reckoning south-southwest 460 miles to their final stop, the Ladyville Airport, servicing Belize City.

As an international requirement, Bohun telexed Regimen de Vuelos de Aeronautica Civil de Cuba, in La Habana, Cuba, the day they arrived in Florida, giving them Art's name, the plane's make, model, class and registration number, and his Instrument Flight Rules (IFR) flight plan; after which they received clearance to fly through Fidel Castro's air space the following day, April 7. What followed was enough to unnerve the most seasoned combat pilot.

Once they reached cruising altitude of 14,800 feet, the island of Cuba was clearly visible 108 miles due south. Bohun radioed Havana once they had reached their first checkpoint, and Havana responded with clearance to proceed. As they approached the island and checkpoint number two, just northeast of Varadero and in line with the Isle of Pines, an official at the Havana International Airport came on the air. "IWQ [Williams' plane] please stand by while we check your credentials." Having already received clearance to enter Cuban airspace, Williams found their request annoying, but he did as they requested and pulled his small plane into a circling pattern.

Bohun clearly recalls the event. "While we were wasting precious fuel in this holding pattern, I noticed two Russian MIGs coming up at us, so I turned to Art and told him 'We have company.' Bohun recognized the planes from Jane's books, the encyclopedia for all military equipment. The MIGs had large intakes and the antenna extended from between the rear wings which were turned downward thirty degrees. One flew on either side of Williams Cessna and waved their wings and then one by one they lowered their wheels and proceeded down towards the old Varadero Airport. They did this twice as the international signal to follow them and land.

Bohun and Williams radioed Air Havana again with their flight number and described what was happening and asked permission to land. Air Havana's response was that they had no record of the IWQ's flight plan and said permission was denied and to stand by. The two jets returned and rushed the plane a couple of times, which sucked all the air out from under the wings, causing the Cessna to tumble around like a paper plane. They dropped 2,000 feet in a heartbeat. After the plane recovered, one of the MIGS moved up in front of it.

Bohun recalled, "We were so close I thought our propeller was going to eat up his exhaust pipe. He then turned on his afterburners, dumping raw kerosene all over our fuselage. The smallest spark would have lit us up like a Roman candle. Both of our radios were on separate frequencies, listening to Havana and Varadero at the same time. The two are internationally monitored frequencies, so we knew the Americans had to be listening. We could hear a Wardair commercial flight taking off from the runway at Havana Airport and I kept cutting in and saying things like 'Why are you doing this? We are Canadians. We don't hate anybody.' They were roughly eighty miles to our west, so we knew they had to be aware of us and of the situation we were in.

"At this point, Art told me to hold on; he was going to show these guys. He pushed the Cessna into a power dive so steep that I jammed my feet up against the dash so I could stay in my seat, at the same time reaching behind me for my life jacket. I thought for sure I was going through the windshield, and whatever was to be left as shark bait was going to be clinging to a life jacket. Art yelled at me, "Get your God-dammed feet off my instrument panel. What kind of soldier were you, you cowardly bastard. Get a grip on yourself." Art was hauling back on the wheel for all he was worth and eventually pulled his plane level at 100 feet off the deck. He told me the jets were unstable at slower speeds and would lose major altitude in turns; therefore, they would never pursue us at such a low elevation.

"Eventually Havana tower came on the air and said, 'IWQ, where are you?' By then Art was so furious he grabbed the microphone out of my hand and said, 'IWQ, it's none of your goddamned government's business where I am. Furthermore, if your bloody air force is so efficient, how come they don't know where the hell I am?'

At that point, a woman's voice admonished Art in clear English, 'IWQ, this is an international net. Please watch your language.' Art started sputtering and snarling into the microphone. 'I know this is an international net and I know that Wardair's black box is recording this for posterity. I also know the Americans are monitoring this frequency. I want everyone to know exactly what you are doing.' He then proceeded to describe the ongoing events in detail all the while sounding like a World War II radio reporter. He was calling them all Cuban murderers who were acting like pirates on the high seas."

Williams and Bohun fixed their heading back towards St. Petersburg. Once on the ground, Williams had the plane refueled for the morning, then got a motel so he could get some sleep while Bohun went to a pub next door called the Stock Market and got hammered. The next morning, anxious to get underway, the two took off with IFR [flight by instrumentation verses visual orientation to the ground] clearance in hand, and as they started to climb, Art turned to Bohun with an odd look on his face and said something must be wrong with his two fuel gauges. He had paid to have the plane filled up the night before, but the gauges were showing empty. Bohun immediately radioed St. Petersburg Airport and requested emergency clearance to return. They had landed the night before with some fuel remaining in their tanks and yet when they had just taken off they were running on vapors. Believing someone had siphoned out all their remaining fuel during the night and knowing the issue with the Cubans would have been within earshot of the American radios, plus the fact that they had done nothing, Bohun and Williams figured the circumstances were far too coincidental to discount as anything other than attempted murder. Art tracked down the guy who had filled his plane the night before. After humming and hawing, the guy suggested he must have filled up the wrong plane.

On our second day flying back, Bohun and Williams found themselves in the middle of a lightning storm somewhere over the New Mexico desert. What started out as little cumulus clouds, quickly turned into a dark dust storm, with twisters and lightning dropping around the plane. Because the storm was moving along at the same speed as they were travelling, Art turned to IFR. No matter how far they went, they just couldn't seem to outrun it. According to Bohun, "Art just kept boogying along. Just as we flew out of it over Cheyenne, Wyoming, Art was making his turn on our approach to set down for the night and blip! blip! blip! the motor quit. He had just switched on the second fuel tank but there had been an airlock in the line from having had it siphoned out in St. Petersburg. He never got flustered but got her started again just as we set her down on the assigned runway."

On his return home, Williams contacted the Nanaimo Free Press with regards to the Cuban incident. The article quoted Williams, "We were moving towards St. Petersburg, Florida and about 15 minutes out of Cuban airspace before we emerged from the low-level fog. The two MIGs were right up above me waiting like a couple of vultures following the shadow of their prey below. It was as though their coffee break was now over and they just came down and took up where they had left off. After repeatedly swooping down we were forced into a dive where we leveled out at a hundred feet above the ocean surface. There we stayed following a thirty-minute dogfight for the remaining fifty-two miles to the Florida mainland. I was pretty confident the MIGs would not be able to maneuver below me at that elevation." Williams gave much of the credit for their survival to his training during the Second World War as a British glider pilot, a fact not substantiated by his military records.

Some have suggested the entire event was an easier way for the Canadian government to rid itself of such a troublesome man. A diplomatic IOU is much easier to negotiate than an attempt to wrestle someone to the ground through the judicial system.

By April 28, 1977 neither Williams nor Bohun had received a formal response to their registered complaint to Ottawa. The only statement the feds were prepared to make was that the Cuban story differed from Williams'. "At least they [the Cubans] do admit that there was an incident, and that is surprising," said Williams. Ottawa confirmed that the Canadian ambassador in Cuba had been asked to make inquiries of the incident "near Cuban air space." Bohun went to Ottawa to confront External Affairs, pointing out that the entire event had been taped on the Wardair flight recorder, but "the bureaucrat smiled and assured me that tape in question had been inadvertently erased by a later landing."

Undaunted, the two men made a second, more successful trip to Belize later that year. As before, they flew in Williams' Cessna, but this time Bohun took along his twenty-year-old girlfriend, Sue Townsend. They flew out of Nanaimo's Cassidy Airport on August 6, 1977, stopping for the night in Baker, Oregon before moving on to the El Paso Flying Club in Texas. When they returned to their plane in the morning, ready to set out across the water to Belize, they found someone had removed the nose cone. Without it they were going nowhere, and a replacement was a week away. Hence they took a commercial flight the rest of the way and spent the better part of two weeks at the Fort George Hotel in Belize City. They hired a driver by the name of Hilly Barrow who drove them to Belmopan, the capital of Belize, to Orange Walk in the north, to San Creek and Hattieville, which was set up to house the victims of Hurricane Hatti, but when they were there it was overrun by hippies.

Bohun clarifies, "Belize was part of the British Commonwealth, and at that time you could buy 500 acres for $50,000, so in our minds it made for an ideal place to live. Art went off while I knocked on doors to see what business opportunities there were. One of the banks referred me to the industrial development department of the government, who took a keen interest in helping us get set up with tax breaks."

Sue remembered, "Art had a lot of paperwork with him, and I saw one sheet of paper with all the names of government officials on it. Most of the time we were there, the guys went their separate ways and I played the part of a tourist. They gave me some spending money so I was happy. I didn't much worry myself as to what they were doing. I was just along for the ride. Art did, however, take a fair number of photos of buildings. By the time we caught a commercial flight back to our little plane, it had been repaired. The guys were so bagged, that once we were aloft, Art handed me a piece of paper with the bearings on it and I kept us on course while they nodded off. My father was a pilot so I had a good understanding of my way around an aircraft. As it was, I retraced our steps, except twice I wandered into restricted military air space. US fighter jets came up alongside us, but I would wave at them and then veer away from the area. Being blond didn't hurt."

While Bohun remains adamant that the trip was only for investigating future business opportunities, he has been unable or unwilling to state with conviction, that Williams was not transporting a large sum of his drug money to an off-shore account. Having gone their separate ways during the day, the question also remains as to whether Williams had purchased a hiding place. Both the subject of land values and the means of moving money offshore had been table conversation prior to their departure.

Paul Jackson 1994
Credit: Paul Jackson

Art's plane IWQ on remote beach
Credit: Daniel Ferguson

Art's Cessna 150 with Ray Ridge
Credit: Daniel Ferguson

Don Bohun pointing out damage to IWQ following Cuban incident
Credit: Vancouver Sun

CHAPTER 14:

THE MOLE

Over time my objective dimmed and I simply fell in love with the
power. It was just plain old greed.

—E752

The loss of the mountain lab did not appear to dent the flow of MDA
on the streets. Kary had no doubt another lab was in full operation
elsewhere. In fact, Williams and Elliott had seven other labs working
independently: the one they blew up, two located in a creek upstream
of the Mount Brenton cabin, one on Swallowfield Road, one on Elliott's
property on Old Cowichan Lake Road, two operating in boats offshore,
plus the primary lab on Art's property. Losing one was nothing more
than a hiccup within the course of events.

In the last few months of 1976, around the time the cops were investigating the set-up on Mount Brenton, the RCMP began working a
different angle: infiltrating Williams' operation from the procurement
end. They pinned their hopes on someone they identified as "E752",
someone they stated was an unpaid informant. Only a few men in the

department knew of his existence, and they decided that for the benefit of the case, it would remain that way.

Working undercover in Narcotics is like working in a cesspool. If you find it difficult to lie and cheat, you don't survive. If it is not your given trait, you must learn quickly that in order to penetrate the organization, the end justifies the means. The undercover agent needs to have a certain psyche within his or her head coupled with a lack of moral fiber. You soon become adept at making black look like white. Successful moles become the best salesmen and con men in the world as lies and deceit become their forte.

For the RCMP, E752 was all that and more. He was manipulative, independent, resourceful and as energetic as a street dog. He had learned the art of the deal at an early age on the streets. He hated publicity because it threatened his work and violated his personal code of ethics. He believed that things happened for a reason and there was no such thing as coincidence. To miss the smallest detail would eventually invite a bullet to the head and that would end his career.

The RCMP wanted E752 to entrap Williams and his entourage while they were active in the production and sale of MDA. As the informant explained later, his principle motivation for becoming involved was to remove his competition from the street so he could move in and assume their territory without fear of reprisal. "The cops just didn't understand my motivation," E752 would reveal later. "I started working with them [the cops] to avenge the death of my older brother. My brother had gotten mixed up with the wrong people and one of the fellows he was dealing with took a mind to end his life early. My objective from that point on was to see that the life of the fellow who killed my brother ended before he planned it. By working with the cops, I had a license to make the contacts I needed which would lead me to the fellow I wanted. By some stroke of luck, he ended up dying at the hands of someone else. Over time my objective dimmed and I simply fell in love with the power. It was just plain old greed."

The Victoria Times newspaper reported the informant, "had first struck up a relationship with Kary while he was facing an outstanding charge for armed robbery. As an incentive to join forces with the RCMP, Kary pulled a few strings and the charges were dropped." The informant stated he had orchestrated the conviction of fifteen to twenty people by the time he got involved with Williams, and each conviction earned him a fresh meal ticket on the front lines of the underworld's buffet.

E752 was born in the early 1950s and grew up in Quebec before moving to the West Coast in 1971. "I never made it through grade nine. The teacher caught me smoking in school and said if I were willing to take four straps, then he wouldn't tell my parents. I endured the four straps but he still told my parents, so I figured I had learned all I was going to learn in school and left. My parents were caring and nurturing folk but their marriage was disastrous. With all that happened in my early years, my personality led me to revolt against all that stood in my way."

He had become practiced working cautiously as if surrounded by pockets of quicksand. "I found I was able to look without seeing. I practiced all the possibilities of mental evasion I could while staying adrift in what I considered to be a sea of undefined shadows, and yet remaining alert to what dangers were around me. It becomes a state of mind after a while where a laugh or a smile is simply the sheathing for someone's true emotions."

Fluent in five languages, E752 was no stranger to the dark side of life. He set himself up prior to his involvement in the Williams case as a bona fide purveyor of hashish, marijuana and cocaine and boasted at having extensive connections with the Hell's Angels throughout Canada and the United States. According to Kary, he had worked for the RCMP in Quebec, Prince George and Kamloops before taking up space in Ladysmith, and from the outcome of those cases, they considered him reliable. Besides the risk associated with his makeup, the Mounties had little else to go on, and based on their lack of success to date, they felt they had nothing to lose.

Not long after E752 arrived in Ladysmith, he met Dewy Babcock, a local fellow who knew everyone who mattered. Dewy introduced him to the Island players, and in time he came to realize that E752 wasn't a man you wanted to mess with. As Dewy recalls, "There was this time when he and I were coming out of the Lantzville Pub and another guy just happened to be walking towards us from the service station next door. My new friend walked straight up to him, pulled out a 9 mm from his hip that I never knew he had, and pistol-whipped the guy to the ground. He then drove the muzzle of the gun into this guy's head while yelling for everyone to hear, 'Give me the money.' This was in broad daylight. There was no doubt in my mind that he would have wasted the guy if he felt it was necessary."

The police wanted their mole to work slowly into Williams' life and ask him for an opportunity to build a clandestine MDA lab of his own. As it turns out, the mole had been introduced to Williams approximately a year earlier by Don Bohun since he and Bohun frequented the same marina. The two socialized a fair bit and one day they happened to be in a restaurant when Williams walked in.

After being enlisted by the RCMP and feeling that he couldn't simply walk up to Williams and get things rolling, E752 contacted Bohun and suggested to him that he had a source for gelatin caps and wondered if he knew of someone who would be interested. He knew that Bohun was tight with Williams and that, likely, the message would find its way to his target.

Elliott states he had a feeling that E752 was a rat right from the start. While Art had much the same notion, he wanted to play with him just the same. However, when E752 asked for an opportunity to become involved in the production of MDA, Williams saw no room for flexibility and refused him flatly. Both Williams and Elliott only dealt with a few hand-selected people. If you were someone Williams considered trustworthy there remained an open invitation to become an active participant. At the same time, he didn't hold it against anyone for not participating. Happy Laffin recalls, "He invited me to get involved, saying I would make millions, but I wanted nothing to do with it. Art just accepted my decision and it didn't seem to affect our relationship."

Although E752 seemed suspect, the capsules he was offering were vital to the ongoing trade. The authorities regulated sales of capsules so that only a handful could be purchased at one time by the public, so when E752 told Williams that he could provide him with a quantity of #4 gelatin capsules, Williams took the bait. He agreed to pay $30 per thousand and ordered a million.

Elliott was concerned about the deal because the price was so low. As it was, Elliott had a continuing relationship with a drug store pharmacist in Vancouver who was supplying him with capsules in bulk. The pharmacist would put the capsules in a thirty-gallon barrel out the back door of his shop. Elliott would watch for the barrel and then go by after hours and pick them up. The pharmacist charged Elliott 10 percent over his purchase price, and that was fair for both. Elliott had seen the invoicing so he knew what they cost the parmacist, and the caps that E752 was offering were priced well below that. Besides the ridiculously low price, E752's capsules looked tainted or opaque. His excuse was that they had been shipped a long way. Elliott didn't buy that either because his supplier's capsules were shipped a long way as well, and he told E752 as much. But, Elliott stated, "Art was convinced that he could outsmart the cops if they were involved, so he went ahead with the purchase. Art was a brilliant guy," he added, "but there were times when he lacked street smarts."

The authorities felt confident Art would be a fool to pass up a pipeline when offered. The cops knew that Williams was so desperate for the tiny containers that he had designed a capsule-making machine, which he was in the process of building. They knew that if the lack of supply pushed Williams to realize a patent in his machine, they would have a whole new set of problems to deal with. There was no law against manufacturing and distributing capsules, and they feared that if he succeeded in its creation, he could feed the underground without any worry of legal reprisal.

At 7 p.m. on February 4, 1977, Kary met with his informant in a Nanaimo motel to give him 25,000 capsules. So, they could be identified at a later date, the RCMP's chemist, Richard Bergman, came up with a mixture of ASA (Aspirin) and caffeine in ordinary ethanol. When this was sprayed on an empty shell and allowed to dry, it could only be detected when viewed under an ultraviolet light. Before Kary gave his informant the bundle of caps, he searched the informant and his truck.

(This became the practice each time the RCMP orchestrated a drop or transfer.)

Williams had agreed to meet his new supplier in a field located at the north end of the Nanaimo/Cassidy Airfield, accessible from Haslam Road. From a distance, Kary watched Williams' green Chevy 4 x 4 pull up beside the informant's red Ford pickup. Everything appeared to be going well when, for no apparent reason, Williams drove out of the field, back onto the road and towards where Kary was parked. Kary figured he and possibly his informant's cover had been blown, and then Williams turned and drove back to the Ford pickup. Williams was displaying the same suspicious traits he had shown in October 1972 while collecting the shipment of chemicals from the Vancouver warehouse and this made Kary nervous.

When the transfer was complete, Williams drove off in the opposite direction from the highway. As Kary proceeded to the transfer point, he found his mole walking back towards the highway. Williams had directed his supplier to a wet area just off the side of the road where he was certain to become stuck. If the transfer went sour, Williams was going to insure any uninvited visitors would end up mired in the mud alongside their informant. Kary searched the truck to insure the transfer had taken place and then drove his informant to Ladysmith so he could call a wrecker.

E752 had been promised $1,075 for the capsules, so the next morning, on the main street of Ladysmith he met Williams as instructed and received payment in full. Kary allowed his informant to keep the money, a deal which would continue for the duration of the sting.

With a supply of capsules from the RCMP, Elliott and Williams ramped up MDA production and distribution. The pair constantly changed their drop location. Elliot said, "We never used the same spot when it came to picking up the money. This way we knew the feds would have a difficult time gaining a conviction on trafficking. We always left coded messages with the drop as to where the next one would be. We also worked a deal with a local gas station and a restaurant to act as drop points in exchange for a commission. They were small businesses and welcomed the added cash flow."

Daniel Ferguson, Shirley's son, adds, "Art was always trying to find a creative way to move his MDA. I remember on one occasion he had milled this cylinder on his lathe that had a section that screwed off, leaving a cavity in which he could place his stash. It was machined so perfectly that you couldn't see where it came apart. It just looked like a solid chunk of aluminum." Williams clothed every segment of a deal in a veil of secrecy.

Arrests for trafficking MDA were being made in all points of the Pacific Northwest. After each arrest, the RCMP sent the capsules to their lab in Vancouver and often they proved to be the same ones Williams had purchased from the informant. The police, however, needed more evidence to guarantee a conviction. What they needed was a lab.

CHAPTER 15:

CAT AND MOUSE

Our whole investigation was geared towards getting the lab.

—Sgt. Bob Hawkes

During the latter part of February, E752 met with Art at the old Cassidy Inn on several occasions to discuss further deliveries of the caps and the acquisition of MDA. Eventually Williams provided E752 with a quarter-ounce sample of MDA in a brown plastic bag. RCMP chemists found it to be 22 percent pure.

On February 24, 1977, Kary sprayed an additional 67,000 capsules for delivery. After testing a few in a ferric chloride solution, they turned purple, indicating the caffeine solution had adhered. The following day, Kary turned over a medium-sized steamer trunk containing a large green garbage bag filled with the little treasures to his informant. The transfer took place in the parking lot of the Newton Inn in Surrey, on the outskirts of Vancouver, BC. As prearranged, E752 met Williams at the Delta Air Park at 9:40 a.m. the same day.

Punctual as usual, Williams' Cessna taxied up to the fuel pumps where he and the informant spoke. After a few minutes, they moved into the adjoining coffee shop. Kary noted the two spent a half hour together, after which Williams took possession of the trunk and its contents. Williams agreed to pay later and flew off. Within two days, another exchange of 50,000 capsules took place at the same location along Haslam Road where the informant had become stuck in the mud.

Williams finally decided to trust his contact and agreed to sell E752 half a pound of raw uncut MDA paste for $4,500. Kary was ecstatic. As Williams had instructed, E752 met his plane at 5 p.m. on March 27 at the Delta Air Park. By the time his plane had touched down, the RCMP had their cameras trained from every vantage point to capture the moment. Kary watched as the plane taxied up to their informant's gold-colored Olds Cutlass. Dale Elliott climbed out of the Cessna's passenger side and slid into the Cutlass. The two drove off as Williams returned to the air.

Had Williams or Elliott looked back, they would have seen a dozen officers scrambling in every direction to retrieve their vehicles. The armada of unmarked 76 Ford Galaxies rolling out of the airport looked like a sequel to the movie Cannonball Run. At a safe distance they followed the Cutlass to the Langley Airport, some fifteen miles to the east, where Williams' plane sat idling at the end of the tarmac. Rather than driving out onto the strip, Elliott directed E752 to turn right at the entrance to the airport and pull into the driveway of a vacant house approximately 150 yards further down the road.

Elliott explains, "Art and I had flown in earlier that day and we found this vacant house with all kinds of junk in the yard. I stashed the paste under a wooden box after which we flew back to Delta Airport, where we met him [E752]. We knew this arrangement would frustrate the cops if they were set up to watch us land. After I jumped into the Cutlass, I could see the rat checking his mirror seeming very distracted. I was convinced he had something going on. When we got to the vacant house, I pointed to the box, but E752 wanted me to get out of the car and show him the MDA which threw up more red flags. I wasn't about to get suckered into that so I refused and told him to take me to the Langley Airport, where I knew Art would be waiting. After that he could retrace his steps and collect it for himself."

When dropped at the airport, the RCMP watched as Elliott sauntered across the tarmac, hoisted himself into the right side of Williams' plane, and the two took off.

After catching up with his mole, Kary drove with him over to the vacant home and retrieved what appeared to be half a pound of MDA. By then there was no doubt in the authorities' minds that another lab existed: this MDA was fresh, wet and sticky to the touch. Kary took a small sample for testing and gave the remainder to the informant to do with as he wished. (It took five months for the Vancouver Crime Lab to give Kary a positive identification on the small sample of MDA taken from the informant. Every department interpreted priorities differently. One toxicologist recorded that Williams' MDA was different than Elliot's. He stated, every chemist had his own chemical signature.)

Two days later at 7 p.m. on March 29, 1977, Kary met with his informant and again searched his car and person before giving him $4,500 in marked bills to pay for the MDA he had already received. Kary observed the transfer of money the same day to Williams at 7:30 p.m. in the parking lot of the Cassidy Inn. Everything was coming together as planned.

On April 15, Kary met his informant at the Island Hall in Parksville and gave him a further 100,000 capsules. Two days later Williams took possession of the caps and insisted that the transfer of one pound of MDA would take place that evening at the Qualicum Beach Airport.

Adding a twist to the game, E752 suggested to Art that the MDA could be dropped from his plane into an abandoned mining claim that the mole owned on the outskirts of Qualicum Village. He thought the suggestion would offer Williams an added sense of control. In his own words: "I had this land that I had scammed off the E&N Railway, so I figured if I could use it to make the plan intriguing enough, he wouldn't turn it down." So at 5 p.m. on the 17th, Kary and Constable Parfeniuk hid in the brush surrounding the drop site and waited patiently for Williams' arrival as their informant made his way out into the center of a clearing.

Williams had been watched by the cops from the moment he took off from the Cassidy/Nanaimo Airport. The sky was mostly cloudy as he flew north. Passing slowly over the drop site, he returned a few minutes later, flying about a hundred feet above the tops of the trees. Everyone could see an arm clutching a large green plastic garbage bag sticking out from the passenger side door, which they believed belonged to Ray Ridge. Ray Ridge's wife, Bev Nicholls, clarified, "A large portion of the case against Ray Ridge was hinged on the witnesses' testimony that they saw him lean out of the plane and drop the bag of MDA. Fact is it wasn't Ray. It was his brother Dave who was doing the drop with Art that day. Being the type of guy he was, Ray just kept his mouth shut and took the rap for his brother." After the drop, Williams banked sharply and pushed his plane back towards the Cassidy Airport. As it happened, Dave missed the mark by a considerable distance, nearly hitting Parfeniuk in the head. E752 scurried to retrieve the parcel, and handed it to Kary.

Everything had gone like clockwork. Inside the garbage bag Kary found four plastic bags double-wrapped and knotted. In each of the four inner parcels he found two opaque plastic bags, the contents of which were wrapped in sheets of the April 12 edition of the Nanaimo Daily Free Press. Kary reported that the total accumulated weight was roughly one pound. It was tan in color, very gooey and smelled strongly of ether or benzene. Kary scooped roughly thirty grams with his pocketknife and placed it in a pill vial, handing the remainder back to his mole so he could distribute it to his contacts on the mainland.

The chemical analysis came back positive at 55 percent pure. The RCMP were surprised at how the purity had increased so abruptly in just a matter of months. Later they would learn that Williams and Elliott had tweaked the formula with each new batch, thus improving its purity. Elliott put it: "While we knew we were the primary supplier for the west coast, we also knew that before long other chemists would take up the craft. When that happens there would be so much stuff around that if we weren't pushing hard to be the best, our market share would lose interest."

The RCMP had done everything in its power to lead Williams to believe that he was in control. They knew that Williams' contempt for them would eventually cause him to slip up, and if he relaxed enough he might become careless and give them the opportunity they were waiting for.

With time running out, a third buy was engineered. As expected, Williams took the bait at a pre-agreed price of $17,000 for two pounds of his best, which police estimated would sell on the street for $350,000. They would leave Williams to work out the details. If nothing else, it would give the RCMP one more opportunity to evaluate how the man thought.

Williams insisted that the plan would unfold on May 5 in the parking lot of the Horseshoe Bay ferry terminal, north of Vancouver.

With the terminal nestled in a small valley, there were only two ways in or out once the transfer had taken place. It was considered an easy site to monitor, with enough activity around the area to render the cops inconspicuous among the crowd of travelers. As the ferry arrived, the officers would stand in the passenger waiting area and parking lot of the terminal, ready to record the moment. Others were on the ferry to monitor Williams in transit. However, the on-board cops soon reported that neither Williams nor any of his soldiers were on board. There was a further wrinkle when Kary discovered that his informant was not waiting for him at the Hyatt Regency in Vancouver, as planned, but was at the Trolls Restaurant in Horseshoe Bay, overlooking the ferry terminal.

Kary raced the ten miles from downtown Vancouver to Horseshoe Bay. As the ferry arrived, E752 walked out of Trolls, got into his car and proceeded down to a private parking lot immediately west of the government docks. Ray Ridge walked up the ramp of a private wharf adjacent to the government dock and got into his car. He then instructed E752 to drive over and park in the ferries' staff parking lot."

Sensing that something might be afoot, Elliott and Ridge had crossed the strait the night before in Elliott's twenty-one-foot Star Craft and stashed the stuff on a rocky outcrop near the government wharf. When it came time, Ridge jumped off the bow of the boat onto the small private wharf located next to the government facility, then proceeded to look for their contact's car in the parking lot as prearranged.

Caught by surprise, the police radios crackled with the question of what they should do next. Trying not to be too obvious, they adjusted their positions so they had an unobstructed view of the red Camaro their informant was driving that day. From the Camaro, the informant could see a cop peering out the back window of a white van, which was sitting across the road, approximately a hundred feet from where Ridge directed him to stop. After a brief conversation, Ridge got out and walked back down towards the wharf. A few minutes later he materialized and leaned into the driver's window, pulled a tightly wrapped green garbage bag, a little bigger than a basketball, from beneath his jacket, and tossed it onto the informant's lap. There was no request for payment. The act was carried out with such indifference that a casual onlooker would have thought it held as much importance as if one was discarding yesterday's newspaper. Ridge always held E572 in contempt and had no time for small talk. His only words were, "Art told me to give you this."

After the transfer, the informant rendezvoused with Kary at the Park Royal Shopping Mall in North Vancouver. He removed the plastic bag from his car and handed it to Kary. Within the outer bag were two smaller ones. Photographs were taken as evidence, as were samples from each bag. Like before, the remainder of the MDA was given to the mole to do with as he wished. He would later comment, "The cops really put themselves in harm's way that day. Rather than wear rubber gloves like they should have, they handled the MDA with their bare hands. It leached into their skin and affected them so badly that neither one of them showed up for work during the following week."

In a matter of days, the bulk of the drop found its way into the bloodstream of city streets, and the profits slid neatly between the folds of the mole's leather wallet.

In court, Kary later justified leaving the bulk of the MDA with his informant saying he didn't want to disrupt the trafficking network that was in operation. In his words, he wanted "[E752] to be able to return to Williams having distributed the contraband and continue his association with Williams and all other persons concerned." In effect, the RCMP's actions provided a known dealer with the means of profiting personally from its sale, which collectively had a street value of nearly one million dollars. In Kary's view, any ruined lives would have to be sacrificed to a greater good. "There is no lack of distributors the likes of E752," Kary explained, "and if you take one of them down, there will always be another to rise up. But if you take down the organizational head, you take down the knowledge of distribution, manufacturing and the entire organization at the same time. You must maintain the flow or risk loss of your informant. Art Williams just superseded all other targets."

In the middle of June 1977, Kary persuaded his mole to start wearing a small recorder, which he would either tape to his underarm or slip into the crotch of his shorts. Unless he felt that his position would be compromised, every meeting he held with the principal players had to be taped. After hours, Kary and his comrades would pore over the tapes, listening for shreds of evidence. While a few the tapes were crisp and clear, they yielded nothing of use. On the other hand, many tapes were nearly impossible to decipher. It was as though the mole had placed his hand over the mic, intentionally muffling the conversation.

Kary often questioned if E752 was his mole inside Williams' organization or a man working the inner core of the RCMP on behalf of Art Williams. Whatever the case, in the end, their mole left them with ample reason to regret their relationship.

In E752's own words, "The whole case was ill-conceived and yet in my opinion it was well funded. I was definitely manipulating them. I would disable the recorder they had wired to the inside of my leg if it was convenient for my needs and yet I was reliable when I saw it was necessary. At times, it was not suitable for the cops to know what Art and I were talking about; hence the continuity of evidence was not always there. I basically refused to wear it when I was meeting with Ridge or Elliott because I feared they would find it. I knew the rules of the game I was playing and it called for immediate extermination of anybody who was known to carry one of those things. I also knew all three of those gentlemen to be capable of just that.

There was one time when I was wired and I went over to Art's house. I let myself in and he and Shirley were getting it on in bed. As I walked through their bedroom door, Shirley jumped out of bed and proceeded to grab my crotch, intimating she wanted to make it a threesome. It is nothing short of a miracle that the back of her hand didn't rub up against the recorder."

Attempting to tighten the noose around Ridge's neck, the RCMP asked their informant to approach him and ask for a sample of fresh MDA to show his clients.

So, he paid Ridge a visit at his home and requested the sample. Ridge went into the back yard and returned with a small quantity from somewhere behind a tree. E752 in turn gave the sample to Kary.

Although the RCMP already had a substantial amount of evidence to convict Williams, Elliott, and Ridge, they felt their case remained circumstantial at best. By then the cost of the investigation was running well into seven digits, but no matter how hard the boys upstairs pushed for a conviction, Kary and Hawkes had no intention of making a move that would allow Williams to slip between the cracks once again. "If we had picked him up," said Hawkes, "he'd be back on the street within a few days and twice as wary of us. Our whole investigation was geared towards getting the lab." Each buy was designed to whet Williams' appetite, lead him towards a more substantial transaction and eventually weaken his resolve until he opened the doors of his lab to their informant.

As for the mole, over the months he had worked with the RCMP, he had remained a dope dealer through and through. In fact, with every month that went by, he became craftier. He sold the MDA that he was given, combined the proceeds with the sale of the capsules and reinvested it in a sizable shipment of Mexican marijuana. It was not enough for him to beat the cops; he had to better the competition as well. The MDA cost him nothing, and it was clearly understood that his sources of distribution were protected by the RCMP. By cutting the MDA with lactose or dextrose, he would realize a handsome source of revenue in the days to follow.

CHAPTER 16:

BUSTED!

I still believe that someone had to have told the cops where that key was.

—Dale Elliott

As the investigation entered its seventh year, orders came down to call it a day. Having consumed millions of dollars and every waking hour for hundreds of men, the wiretaps had gone silent and the RCMP began to fear their investigation had been compromised. Either Williams had found their bugs or the pressure they had applied to the chemical suppliers had dried up his stockpile. In addition, the courts denied an application to extend the wiretaps, which left the team with no choice but to make one last move. According to Kary, "It was better to risk the lack of a conviction against Williams and his crew, than to not have exercised the last opportunity we had available."

At 6:56 on the morning of August 16, 1977, three well-armed teams looked over their plan of attack one last time.

Many of those who knew Ridge considered him a fellow not to be toyed with. During the day, he worked as a driver for a Duncan drywall company. Off hours he was one of the major players in Art Williams' underworld of intrigue. The cops knew that if they could turn him with the threat of jail time, it would increase the chances of convicting the other two.

Ray Ridge was just getting ready to start his day when one team of Mounties forced their way into his Ladysmith home. Unexpected, he submitted to them without resistance. For those who had worked for so long, the victory seemed shallow. To that point, they had come away with nothing more than a minor soldier. The adrenaline that had rushed through their veins ebbed and sank to the pit of their stomachs.

The sun had been up for forty-eight minutes and there was not a cloud in the sky as the ten men moved under the direction of Sergeant Bob Hawkes across Elliott's property on Old Lake Cowichan Road. With military precision, Hawkes set up a perimeter while a bomb expert cleared and leveled the front door of the principle dwelling.

As Elliott's front door hit the floor, his wife and children came out of their bedrooms in full force with baseball bats and fists flying. It took Staples and five of his men to physically bring calm to the home. The balance of his force searched the remaining buildings on the property, ensuring no one interfered.

For all their efforts, Dale Elliott was not to be found. Ingrid disdainfully told the officers that he had spent the night in Duncan with friends. Even with all the high-tech surveillance in use right up until the hour of reckoning, no one had seen him leave. Other than a small amount of MDA that was found in one of the trailers and a few boxes of material evidence, Hawkes' team had again come up empty.

The truth was that Elliott, a light sleeper, had heard the cops driving up his gravel driveway. He'd split out the bedroom window of the house and through the bush to Dave Ridge's place where the two of them hopped in a truck and hit out cross-country, driving through the Chemainus River to the bush out back of Williams' place.

During the evening of the 15th, Ray Ridge and Elliott had finished up a batch of MDA at Art's place. While Elliott cleaned up, Ray hid the MDA in a plastic methanol jug out back of Art's property. By the time, Elliott and Dave Ridge got to it, the cops were milling about only a hundred yards from where it was hidden. Elliott always felt there was something odd about where Ray hid the stash; "It was in plain view, in an open area with nothing but ferns growing up around it. Anyone walking out back of Art's place would have found it." Elliott would often wonder if Ray had been turned. "There were just too many peculiar things connected to his involvement," he said. According to Ridge's wife, Beverly, "I wasn't home at the time of the raid, but I can assure you, Ray would never turn on those close to him. He remained loyal to Art to his dying day."

Leaving Williams' place, Elliott bummed an aluminum runabout with a nine-horse motor and fled to Ruth and Gordon Loomis' place on Pylades Island. According to Ruth, Gordon worked himself up into a real flap over the possibility of being charged with harboring a fugitive. Ruth told Elliott to make his way over to the other side of the island where her girlfriend Doris was renting a cabin and suggested she might take him in. As it turned out, Doris relished the company.

The next morning, at the crack of dawn, Ruth and Gordon Loomis woke up to the sound of their dogs kicking up a terrible fuss. Walking up the path from the beach was a battalion of cops dressed in flak jackets and balaclavas and waving a writ to search their land and buildings. Ruth recalls, "Because the evenings were so warm, I had been sleeping out on my porch in the buff. When I stood up, the whole lot of them just froze in their tracks. I think for a moment they may have lost focus on why they had come to the island." After Ruth, had thrown on a robe and satisfied the police that Dale wasn't there, she told them to stay off the other side of the island, because it was owned by a different person. This they accepted at face value. After they had left, Ruth phoned Doris and told her it would be best for Elliott to hide in the bushes until the cops left the island.

When Doris woke Elliott, he asked her to get rid of his radios and put his stuff in the corner of the cabin. He took off through the woods to the north end of the island. There were helicopters and boats running all around the place, so he found himself quite exposed. From time to time, he had to slide under a log for cover and found that licking leaves quenched his thirst.

By the afternoon, everything had quieted down so he headed back to Ruth's place. By the time Elliott got there, the family was up and they were all playing volleyball and behaving as if nothing had happened. Ruth told Elliott that before the cops sailed back to Chemainus, they had photographed all the boats that were pulled up on their beach for future reference. She suggested to Dale that it would be wise if he left Pylades by some means other than the boat he arrived in.

Taking Ruth's suggestion to heart, Elliott got word to Terry Quinn to bring Elliott's Star Craft over to him. From there he took off for the north end of Thetis Island. Elliott remembers that day, "The wind was blowing pretty hard so I dropped anchor and caught up on my sleep. All I had was a small package of beef jerky to carry me over till I got settled. Once the weather had settled down, I made my way across the straits to the Sunshine Coast, where I sold my Star Craft and bought a thirty-foot cruiser named *Reverence*. It was so riddled with problems that I renamed it *Horrible*."

It didn't take him long to set up house on board. After accumulating a supply of chemicals and glassware, he powered up to Salmon Inlet north of Vancouver. Dale stashed his supplies along the power-line near Bear Point, just west of the Grassy Creek logging camp. A buddy of his had a cabin there with a dock, so as time permitted he moved his stash into it. *Horrible* had a single side-band radio, plus a CB with a booster and VHF. Elliott stated, "Before long the CB crackled my handle, 'Quacker, I know you're out there, pick up.' For those who mattered, most knew how to reach me. Those who didn't know how to keep their mouths shut were kept in the dark."

To everyone's surprise, the Dave Staples' team, who had focused on Art Williams' fortress on Westdowne Road, stole the show. Not only did they get their man but they found what had eluded them all so many times before.

The group of officers, including Tom Townsend, a bomb expert; an alarm technician; Pat Convey, the expert locksmith; a police dog handler and his canine, approached Williams' home slowly and cautiously. Never-ending rumors suggested Williams had a penchant for booby traps. Word was that the laboratory they had covertly entered in 1975 had since been set to blow up with any form of unauthorized entry. Every man on the force respected the brilliance that Williams displayed.

To their surprise, the back door of Williams' home was unlocked. Staples motioned for Townsend to move forward and sweep the entrance while the remainder of his men prepared for their rush in. As it turned out, Williams, Shirley and her two boys were sound asleep. Had it not been for the commotion, they likely would have stayed that way during the entire raid. Hearing the steps of six heavyset men making their way systematically through his home, Williams leapt from his bed naked. Staples said, "Art lunged through the bedroom doorway, and, seeing me, he started screaming, 'You Nazi pigs, I'll sue you, I'll sue you.'" The yelling carried on for the better part of an hour as Staples' men worked their way through the remainder of the building. Not long after Williams started into his tirade, the children woke and began to echo his high-pitched voice.

With a search warrant in hand, the police methodically took every corner of their home apart. Walls were sounded for false cavities, and the flooring was pulled back in a search for trap doors. One member hoisted himself into the attic, while the smallest officer squeezed into the crawl space beneath the house. Nothing was off-limits. Clothing, personal treasures and everything that defined Art and Shirley's life together were on display in hopes that they would reveal a clue. Anything considered to be of interest was catalogued, boxed and removed to a waiting van outside. Williams was asked to get dressed, cuffed and read his rights. After Staples was certain there was nothing further to be found in the home, Williams was transported to the Duncan RCMP detachment, where he was placed in a holding cell a few doors down from Ridge.

While other officers moved from building to building, Williams' estranged wife, Margaret, wisely chose to remain in her cabin just a few yards away. Whether she knew how her husband spent his days mattered little. Staples was certain that she had no intention of saying anything or becoming involved in the seizure that was playing itself out under her nose.

With Williams removed from the house, a degree of composure returned allowing Townsend to move the hundred or so yards between the house and the barn, as they called it, which was the new lab for the BC Institute of Mycology. Though Staples had searched the building in 1975 and come up empty, he felt enough time had passed that some scrap of evidence might have found its way through the two-and-a-half-inch-thick wooden doors.

After Townsend, had swept the front door for trigger devices, he made his way around the outside of the three-story building. The main entrance was secured by an unusual lock the likes of which no one had seen before. An odd-looking device they found tucked under the soffit worked as the key. Just inside the entrance was a clean room, which housed a central vacuum system used to remove dust and dirt from clothing, and to one side hung smocks that the technicians put on before entering the inner laboratory. The interior of the room was eighteen by twenty-two feet and it was spotless. Everything was orderly and precise. There was an assortment of instruments used in the cultivation of mushrooms, and the infant spores were labeled and arranged in a rack, but otherwise it stood much as it did during their earlier visit, revealing nothing that would deprive Williams of his freedom.

By then everyone, except Constable Al Hickman and a fellow officer from the Saanich Municipal Police, had directed their search to the basement area, but nothing was there other than the steam furnace that was used to keep the Institute at a constant temperature.

Staples and his crew were beginning to feel sick. Their time had run out. The Attorney General's department had put them on notice that it intended to shut the investigation down. With so many man-hours involved, they had nothing more than inference to link Williams to the MDA labs that they had already found. They had not been able to witness him handling or transferring the drugs to a second party. Without something of substance, they knew they would have difficulty charging him with a single indictable offence. There was no denying that Elliott was a big fish, and when they found him he would be snared tightly in their web, but Williams remained their primary target. If he wasn't taken down, they all knew it was only a matter of time until another man with the same drive and determination as Elliott stepped up to fill the void as the front man.

By the time they regrouped, Hickman was fiddling with the wrought-iron staircase suspended against the exterior of the building and leading to the attic level. He was stymied by the retractable mechanism attached to the stairway. He pushed and pulled anything that looked as though it was associated. On his final attempt, the counterweights shot up without warning and the stairs dropped like a ton of bricks, barely missing his fellow officer.

Taking the lead, Hickman gingerly climbed to the top of the stairs and then along the catwalk that ran the length of the roof. At the end of the catwalk was a second platform that looked like a drawbridge. It dangled out over the edge of the building and could be dropped by a winch to a point partway down the outside of the structure. With it lowered, Hickman made his way along the bridge until he came to an access into the Institute's attic. As with the front door, it was solid as a rock and secured with locks of Williams' own design. Impatient for the locksmith to arrive, Hickman fumbled around beneath the eaves and, with a stroke of luck, found a large key that resembled something out of medieval times. It opened the lock.

Hickman gazed into an apartment of sorts. There were three small rooms. Two were obviously bedrooms. The first room immediately inside the door contained a small counter with a hot plate, an RV-sized cooler, a toilet, a sink and a small bookshelf with a variety of reading material. If the amount of dust was any indication, he figured it had been sometime since it had been occupied. He was happy to have solved the riddle of the retracting stairs, but one question nagged: Why were there living quarters in such an obscure place?

Hickman scratched his head as others dismantled the room piece by piece. They went through all the books, hoping a clue would fall from between the pages. Other than a few fragments of moldy food in the cooler, they again came up empty. With only tenacity left in their arsenal, they moved all the furniture into the center of the room and began looking for a moveable wall or hidden entrance.

To everyone's pleasure, a section of the wall gave way into what appeared to be a closet or hidden passageway. Affixed to the wall along one side was a series of shelves that held an assortment of interesting items, including a few nondescript pieces of lab equipment. As with all the other rooms they encountered, they were not going to abandon this one without first rearranging it from top to bottom. One of the officers reached high up in the rafters, beneath the thick insulation, and pulled out a plastic bag containing gelatin capsules.

Just as they were about to call it a day, Hickman caught his toe on a metal plate set into the floor. It was about the size of a man's body, and beneath it was a vertical shaft of concrete pipe that supported a metal ladder. With the aid of a flashlight he could see that it dropped two stories to the level of the basement. It appeared obvious they had missed something in the lower area.

Townsend moved in and made his way down the pipe. With his flashlight, he could see a long, narrow passageway leading away from the bottom. The walls, ceiling and floor were all painted matte black and reflected next to no light. The end of the tunnel turned to the right and opened into a small room with shelving along the left side. Behind the shelves, he could see the walls were blank. "Why?" was again the question of the day. Every time they turned a corner, they were left with yet another unanswered question.

Townsend made his way back up the ladder to the apartment level, and then returned to the basement the normal way in hopes of tying the passageway into the building's overall design.

The basement was divided into two distinct areas. The one on the left was large with access via a sliding double door. Its primary function seemed to be that of a workshop, where Williams repaired machinery and other soiled equipment. To the right was a separate room about the size of a single-car garage. Access was gained through an outside door. At the far end of this room sat the boiler, which provided heat for the entire building. Off to the left was the metal ladder he had climbed down not five minutes earlier, but this time he was on the opposite side of it and barred from entering the darkened passageway by the ladder itself. Looking closely at every detail of the fixture, Townsend noticed that one of the rungs was spring-loaded and hinged upwards. As soon as he pulled on that rung, the ladder swung flush against the interior wall, giving free access into the confined passageway he had previously navigated. There had to be a clue in this area, and he was determined to find it.

With only his flashlight, Townsend made his way back down the corridor to the area where the shelving stood against the wall. On his knees and looking upwards, he could make out a hinge connected to the top left corner of the nearest shelf. The space between the two sets of shelves was wide enough that he could reach through and feel what proved to be a bicycle chain running from floor to ceiling. As he pulled on it, a catch released, permitting the shelving unit to swing free of the wall, revealing a three-foot-square steel door set flush into the interior's concrete wall. To the left side of the door, at about knee height and recessed into the door's surface, were two small round holes which Townsend assumed provided access to a lock.

Before he allowed anyone to come into the area, he spent the better part of an hour poking in and around the door looking for an explosive device. As he moved aside, Pat Convey noticed a crudely made pair of twisted iron rods on one of the shelves. He took the rods and stuck one in each of the holes, but nothing happened. Next, he put a rod in one hole and then a second rod in the other still with no results. He then stuck them both into their respective holes at the same time and turned them in unison. There was a faint click and the tumblers dropped free. As it swung open, he could see the door was solid steel and a full six inches thick. He noticed it could also be operated on air pressure because of the high-pressure hose that had been plumbed to the inner latching mechanism.

"I still believe that someone had to have told the cops where that key was," says Dale Elliott. "There were only three of us who knew where it was and they were Art, Ridge and me. I know Art would not have told them and I sure didn't. It was never left out in the open and always hidden on a metal ledge up inside the furnace boiler. We had to reach up inside and above the furnace door, beyond our line of vision to grab it. If the furnace had been operating, that key was always red hot and we had no choice but to drop it on the floor for a few minutes to cool off. The cops would never have found it on their own." In Elliott's opinion, the proverbial finger once again pointed towards Ray Ridge.

The steel door opened into a damp, blackened, four-foot-diameter concrete cylinder sitting on end. A robust man would never have been able to squeeze through the entrance, not only because of its minimal size, but due to its proximity to the floor. Convey could find no light so he had to feel his way around. The cylinder walls were rock hard and cold to his touch. A strange sensation came over him after he forced his way inside and stood up. He realized the cylinder rose six feet and then abruptly ended. With a light, he could see a metal plate similar to that which Hickman had stubbed his toe on in the apartment. On the floor sat a concrete construction block that offered just enough lift to support someone wishing to climb higher. Before foolishness ruined a good day, everyone was ushered away from the area so the bomb expert could take his place.

Townsend gingerly felt around and looked for evidence of a trigger entry. He found none so he pushed up against the plate with both hands. To his surprise, it swung up and away, offering him unrestricted access. With a flashlight in hand he climbed to the top of the cylinder and peered into a twelve-foot-square concrete bunker with a seven-foot ceiling. Word filtered down the line that at last they had found what they had been looking for. One by one his peers picked their way up the cylinder to have a look at the wizardry of the man they had been pursuing for so long.

Beneath a microscope lay twenty-six of the gel caps the RCMP had covertly provided. Off to the side were other caps that Williams had acquired from different sources. From the way, they were placed under the microscope, it appeared Williams had become suspicious and was trying to confirm the caps had not been tampered with. Staples knew that even if the informant had let the cat out of the bag, the way they had marked the caps was so simple that Williams was looking well beyond where he needed to go.

As they closed the lid to the shaft, they could see more clearly the thought that had gone into that portion of the construction. The upper surface of the lid was crisscrossed with levers and hydraulic hoses that ran off toward the nearest wall. As Townsend pulled the hatch closed, it in turn automatically closed the six-inch-thick metal door that gave access to the cylinder. Protruding from the inside wall, a bicycle chain with a simple sprocket and winder attached ran down through the floor. When he gave the winder a turn, the shelving unit in the hallway slid back into its rightful place.

The same ventilation system that kept the mushroom lab free of dust and rich with filtered air also fed this hidden lab. The same ductwork ingeniously concealed a wiring conduit and plumbing that kept the MDA lab operational. A depression in the floor carried away the wastewater and leftover chemicals. The depression flowed into a grate that covered an eighteen-inch-diameter culvert, large enough for an average man to crawl through.

One of the more daring officers ventured down into that pipe. After crawling at an incline for approximately thirty feet, the culvert leveled out. At one point a second shaft came in on the left. He assumed it came from the two-bedroom attic apartment. About sixty feet beyond the point where it leveled, the culvert opened into the bank of the small creek that ran parallel to the back of Williams' property. The opening was hidden by a large clump of blackberries and scrub brush, and not far from the tunnel exit stood the shed that contained a Honda dirt bike and a jerry can of fuel. A few yards upstream of that, the creek flowed through a six-foot-diameter drainage culvert that provided access into the forested area behind his land. From there, anyone who was trying to escape the wrath of the authorities could either walk or ride into the hills until things had cooled down.

At the lab, one of the officers took a sample of water that had splashed across the wall behind the sink. After testing, it came up positive for trace elements of MDA. In truth, no one had believed that Art Williams had built a lab on his own property. Back at the detachment, Staples joined Hawkes and together they paid Williams a visit in his cell, telling him what they had discovered.

Williams offered them nothing more than a defeated grin.

Art's mycology & MDA lab
Credit: Vancouver Sun

Hidden passageway to MDA lab
Credit: Daryl Ashby

Drawbridge to attic of MDA lab
Credit: Vancouver Sun

Shelving that concealed
access to Art's lab
Credit: Daryl Ashby

Hidden access to
Art's lab
Credit: Daryl Ashby

Art's hidden lab
Credit: Vancouver Sun

Escape tunnel from
Art's lab
Credit: Vancouver Sun

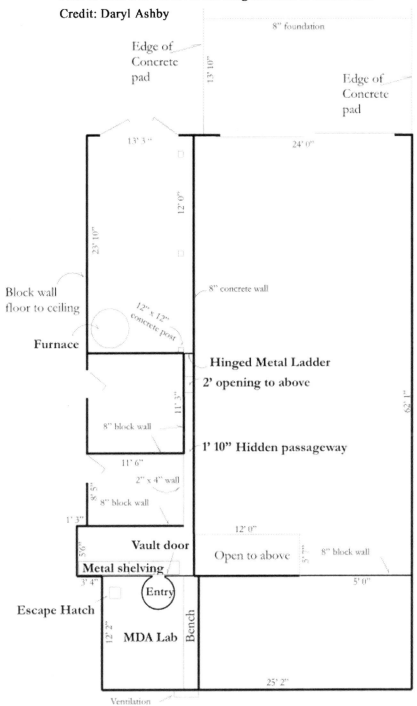

Plan of barn's lower level showing location of hidden lab.
Credit: Daryl Ashby

8" foundation

Edge of
Concrete
pad

13' 10"

Edge of
Concrete
pad

8" foundation

13' 3 "

24' 0"

12' 0"

23' 10"

Block wall
floor to ceiling

8" concrete wall

12" x 12"
concrete post

Furnace

Hinged Metal Ladder

2' opening to above

11' 3"

8" block wall

1' 10" Hidden passageway

11' 6"

2" x 4" wall

8' 5"

8" block wall

1' 3"

62' 1"

12' 0"

5' 6"

Vault door

Open to above

5'

8" block wall

5' 0"

Metal shelving

3' 4"

Entry

Escape Hatch

12' 2"

Bench

MDA Lab

25' 2"

Ventilation

169

CHAPTER 17:

THE END TIMES

He argued his views with his usual overbearing self-assurance and forced a full range of topics upon everyone at the table. He never once mentioned the court case and neither did we. That was the last time we saw him.

—Ruth Dashwood (Art's sister)

August 16, 1977, capped over seven years of work for Dave Staples, Chester Kary, Bob Hawkes, Al Hickman and a score of other officers. They held such a feeling of relief that not one of them could contain their excitement. At last Williams and Ridge were going to go down for a very long time. Williams especially, had enjoyed the luxury of being one step ahead of those he despised, but now his clandestine drug operation was in ruins, and any plans to enjoy a sun-drenched retirement seemed to vanish.

With Elliott, still at large, Arthur Williams and Raymond Ridge were each charged with two counts of conspiracy to traffic in MDA and six counts of possession for the purpose of trafficking in MDA - Hydrochloride.

On August 17, the Victoria Times and its sister newspaper the Colonist ran an article entitled "Seven Arrested in Drug Swoop." The media's interest was so shallow that they lumped the efforts of those seven long years in with the arrest of a couple of small-time dealers of Victoria. Not that Staples and his team were looking for sensational journalism, but the small announcement in the lower corner of the second page hardly reflected the magnitude of the industry that they had brought to its knees. The front-page story in most major publications however headlined with bold, black, two-inch letters running across the top of the page, was the death of Elvis Presley. Despite all the millions of public dollars spent to bring Williams to justice, Presley's death rendered it lesser news.

Williams and Ridge attended a bail hearing at the Duncan County Court on August 17, 1977. The two listened patiently as Crown Counsel Cecil O.D. Branson outlined their nefarious activities. Williams' long-time friend Don Bohun appeared on behalf of the accused. Judge Lance Heard held the gavel.

In such a small community, it was hard to find anyone in the judicial system that had not been exposed to Art Williams or a member of his fraternity. Judge Heard had the benefit of knowing both the subject and the accused, having presided over the preliminary hearing of their 1974 trial. This fact could only hinder their plea.

Branson opened his remarks by petitioning Judge Heard to restrain the two until the formal hearing, stating, "There is sufficient evidence to show that the two had a penchant to commit crimes against humanity." Bohun objected to the petition with a well-scripted three-page rebuttal that painted the two as mischievous choirboys. In response, Branson named Bohun as a co-conspirator, suggesting that conversations between the lawyer, Williams, Ridge, Elliott and the Crown's primary witness, E752, were within spitting distance of criminal activity.

Notwithstanding Bohun's efforts, the two accused were denied bail. Upon appeal, and before two weeks had passed, Ridge had won his bid for release by posting a $2,500 bond. Williams posted a $10,000 bond to secure his freedom, in addition to two sureties of $10,000 to guarantee his appearance at a preliminary hearing, scheduled for November 3, in

Duncan Provincial Court. He knew this rap would be a lot harder to beat than the one in 1973, and even if he were successful, the vultures at Revenue Canada were ready to tear apart what remained of his financial skeleton. Williams left the courthouse knowing his every activity was going to be monitored.

When he returned home, he found every building on his Westdowne Road property in ruins. The RCMP had torn large holes in the cedar walls and ceiling of his mushroom lab and top-floor apartment. All his lab equipment, including that licensed to the Institute of Mycology, plus all related records, had been seized and trucked off to the RCMP lockers for cataloguing and scrutiny.

The preliminary hearing got underway in the Duncan courthouse on November 3 under the watchful eye of Judge R. Moir. This event gave the prosecution a chance to convince the judge that there was enough evidence to justify a trial. E752 was sworn in and run through a gauntlet of questions that highlighted his involvement with Williams, Elliott and Ridge in the production and trafficking of MDA.

The prosecutors intended to work the kinks out of their arguments against Ray Ridge first, as the lesser of the players, with hopes of tightening their case against their primary target, Williams, at some later date.

Sid Simons who replaced Bohun as the defense counsel for all the accused, consumed the greater portion of the court's time bickering over legal procedure in an attempt to see the case thrown out. His basis for such a request was the fact that the Crown's primary witness was clearly more threatening to public safety than the accused.

At the close of the proceedings, Judge Moir concluded that there was overwhelming evidence in support of moving ahead, so the case would be heard, but in a higher court. If the matter affected Williams in any way, nothing in his demeanor made it obvious.

As the months passed, the Mounties recorded Williams' day-to-day movements and watched as his personal flight records tallied a staggering number of hours. Trouble for Williams didn't remain behind the courtroom doors but followed him as he flew into the Vancouver International Airport on October 8, 1977.

A complaint was registered for some perceived violations related to his method of landing at 9:33 a.m. that day. Per the complaint, Williams "failed to obtain clearance to land and failed to obtain clearance to cross a runway in use after landing." He also "failed to contact the controller as instructed by the ATC agency, on the specified frequency upon entry into the PCz."

The complaint further charged that the "airport controller did not observe the aircraft until after it had landed without clearance on runway 08. Pilot of GIWQ had previously contacted the tower initially on 124.0 MHz and obtained instruction to contact the tower on frequency 118.7. No call was received by the tower on 118.7, but the authorities acknowledged it is possible that such a radio transmission could have been blocked by another transmission using that band width. The complaint stated the pilot proceeded to the airport and landed during busy traffic conditions without clearance. After landing, the pilot did not respond to attempts by the ground controller to contact the aircraft and subsequently crossed another runway in use without clearance."

Williams again illustrated his attitude towards authority on November 18, 1977, by responding to the charges on Inkster Aircraft letterhead to C.P. Moran, the regional superintendent of air regulations:

"The report referred to is incorrect if it indicates any improper action on the part of myself as pilot in command.

"The situation referred to occurred as a result of air traffic control losing track of inbound traffic. Our aircraft, GIWQ was given clearance to land and the pilot [Williams] chose to land long in order to avoid wake turbulence from the aircraft landing ahead.

"I assume that air traffic control, having cleared IWQ to land lost sight of the aircraft and authorized another plane to taxi to position at the time IWQ was landing. Since IWQ was landing long, I had no knowledge of the plane taxiing to position other than from monitoring air traffic control, but was advised by my passenger Mr. Bohun, that such an incident had occurred just at touchdown.

"The position then was this: the live side of the runway was very active. The dead side was also, due to inbound traffic on a cross runway. Planes were departing ahead and voice communications were impossible because air traffic control was releasing the traffic ahead. In view of the fact that the plane behind was holding on the runway, it was dangerous to depart and in any event, forbidden to overshoot to the live side.

"It was dangerous to overshoot on the dead side and impossible to overshoot straight ahead due to departing traffic.

"With instructions to keep in close, it was clear to me what was the safest thing to do, in the few seconds available to make such a decision.

"If this constitutes a breach of regulations, do I understand you to suggest that the regulations are inviolate no matter how dangerous compliance would be?

"Yours truly,

Arthur J. Williams"

In the months that followed his bid for freedom, Williams busied himself on a 110-acre parcel of land in South Wellington, south of Nanaimo, which he had purchased in 1973. The authorities did not pay too much attention to his activities there, other than to note that he and Shirley had put in a garden and spent many hours tending it. Sometime prior to the raid, Williams, with the help of Lou Brown, had built a large Quonset hut, or metal equipment shed, on the sixty-acre portion held by the BC Institute of Mycology. The RCMP had noted this but did not seem to concern themselves about its purpose.

Unbeknownst to Williams, the RCMP had cultivated a second informant. Stanley Cross had become a bona fide heroin addict, and to support his habit he had turned to trafficking the very poison that held him captive. Cross came from Williams' tight circle of friends. Williams, Cross and Ralph Harris had jointly purchased the airframe for a small helicopter, and, according to Elliott the three had intended to assemble it there on the South Wellington property.

Corporal Jerry Moloci had picked Cross up for trafficking in heroin and cocaine on behalf of the 101 Knights, and he made certain Cross understood that he was going down for some hard time if he didn't cooperate. In exchange for turning informant and testifying against all those involved, Cross was assured protection and that all the pending charges would be dropped. As Moloci said, "While he was more connected to the bikers, we figured he had to know something about Art's lab, and with nothing else going for us at the time, we pressed him for all that he knew." It didn't take Cross long to organize his priorities. His friendship with Williams would have to be sacrificed to maintain his freedom. "Stanley didn't know for sure, but he figured that small room in the basement which didn't have a door may be what we were looking for."

In the end, Cross's information about Williams and his crew was minimal in comparison to the evidence he brought against the leadership of the 101 Knights. While Cross figures the leaders of the bike gang unwittingly brought about their own demise, word on the street suggested they saw it differently, and proceeded to place a sizable bounty on his head with no specified expiry date.

When that news filtered down to Moloci, he took every precaution possible to protect his witness, regardless of the cost. In the 1970s there was no government-sponsored witness protection program, so Moloci created one. With an eye for detail, he concocted an alias for Cross and procured a new Social Security number, got him involved in a methadone program and gave him enough cash to relocate himself and his family to friendlier soil. Once settled, Cross could shake off the devil and stay clean as he made the best of his second chance.

Since then, Cross has stated that he would have done things differently if he had to do it again. While Moloci has remained a trusted friend, Cross states, "I would take account for my own actions if I had a chance to do it all over again. I would have done my eight to ten years and then built a new life after I got out. This looking over my shoulder has taken its toll. Even though it has been thirty years, I still have to be cautious." He states that through all his foolishness, his wife of twenty-seven years has stuck with him. "She is the best thing that has ever happened to me."

Art Williams' relationship with his sister Ruth had gone steadily downhill since the day he walked out on Margaret. Interactions between them were limited to one or two visits a year (he never missed Christmas Eve). One night following the preliminary hearing, Ruth and her husband were paying Margaret a social call when Art walked in without notice. "He was his old self," Ruth said. "He argued his views with his usual overbearing self-assurance and forced upon everyone at the table a full range of topics. He never once mentioned the court case, and neither did we. That was the last time we saw him."

Terry & Daniel Ferguson leaving
Wellington Quonset Hut
Credit: Daniel Ferguson

Jerry Miloci working undercover
Credit: Jerry Miloci

CHAPTER 18:

OUT OF CONTROL

To me the invitation just seemed suspicious enough to suggest that
he was organizing some sort of alibi for the event that followed.

—Bev Nicholls

With minor exceptions, November 30, 1977, started out much like any other day in the life of Arthur Williams. Since his two-week confinement, he had left the authorities with the illusion that he had distanced himself from those he referred to as his close circle of friends. As far as the RCMP could tell, there was no evidence that he continued to dabble in the drug trade; rather, he seemed preoccupied around his Ladysmith homestead and on his acreage south of Nanaimo.

"His temperament didn't seem to change much," recalls Allen Dashwood. "I do however recall one instance where he felt he needed to implant in me a sense of responsibility while employing a shock value as only he could. Stanley Cross and I were working for him by clearing some land behind his home. We were using his backhoe, and at the end of the day we put his double-headed axe in the front bucket and drove it back to the house. Arthur met us in route and as soon as he noticed the axe in the bucket he flew into a tirade. During the foray, he reached down, picked up the axe and swung it around and around his head, launching it to some far corner of his property. Stanley and I didn't know what to say, but it impressed on us that it was not good common sense to lay a sharp axe against the steel sides of a bucket. On the conclusion of his demonstration, we were invited into the house for a cup of tea as though nothing had happened."

Shirley Ferguson said, on the evening of November 29th, Art pored through a number of legal journals that he had on loan from the Nanaimo Library. When he found a relevant defense point, he immediately called his new lawyer, Sid Simons, at his home in Vancouver and insisted on a meeting the following day.

Next, he called Ray Ridge and asked him to fly over to Vancouver with him. Ray agreed, but early the next morning, Art called him back and rescinded the invitation saying he knew that Ray had a cook underway and that he couldn't go because he had to take care of it. (A cook is a slang word for the final stage of bringing the MDA into a pasty form.) Ray's wife Bev Nicholls thinks there was more to the story. In her words, "Art knew Ray had this cook on the go the night before, and it would have been nothing for him to have one of the other fellows take care of it, but he didn't. I'm still a bit miffed as to why Art asked him to fly over in the first place when he knew he would insist on him staying back. It wasn't a matter of Art being absentminded; he never forgot anything. He had a mind like a steel trap. To me the invitation just seemed suspicious enough to suggest that he was organizing some sort of alibi for the event that followed."

Ridge did however drive Williams to the Cassidy Airport as he had done many times before. Williams' Cessna sat off to the side of the tarmac, where he had left it. After removing the blocks from the wheels and the straps that secured the wing tips to the ground, he checked all the fluids and then taxied over to the fuel pumps, where he topped up the tanks. He ran through his precautionary checklist, taxied to the north end of the runway and brought the engine speed up in preparation for takeoff.

The skies were overcast, with a 10,000-foot ceiling, and temperatures hovered around 6 degrees Celsius, rendering it a suitable day for a short hop but questionable for anything more. Visibility was limited to just over eleven kilometers, and the wind speed was moderate at nine kilometers from the northeast. While the forecast had suggested light winds and possible showers during the latter part of the evening, the flight went off without a hitch, and Williams was soon greeting Simons at the Vancouver Airport's south terminal.

For this trial, Williams had decided that, rather than relying on his local lawyer and trusted friend Don Bohun, he wanted a lawyer who had proven himself proficient in navigating the inner workings of the B.C. Supreme Court. He had chosen Sid B. Simons, considered by his peers to be hard-nosed and unrelenting. As a defense lawyer, Simons had sharpened his wits on the arguments of numerous high-paid, big-city lawyers. When he was fresh out of UBC he articled with Harry Rankin, the loud, profane, bombastic socialist who spent twenty-four years as a city councilor for Vancouver. It was under Rankin that Simons felt the calling to fight for the rights of the underdog, the tenant who had been gouged, the defendant who was being railroaded or the Native Indian no one would believe. He became so successful in helping some of the most hopeless cases slide through the judicial web that he was soon referred to as Slippery Sid.

Sid Simons was much the same height as Williams, and for that reason it was joked that he would be well-suited to see eye to eye with his client's unique take on the law. In fact, he stood five foot ten, with piercing hazel eyes, and he sported a full beard that was closely cropped to complement his thick black hair. Every barrister has his own trait; Simons' was to fiddle with his glasses while eyeballing those he questioned to unsettle them. He had nearly twenty years of practice when he took on Williams' case, so he was no stranger to conflict. "I could not abide cops who would lie to tie things together in court, and I frequently found those that did." Simons had the single-mindedness of a man certain of his own convictions and wouldn't allow personal aspirations to alter his professional stance.

When it came to Williams, Simons was determined not to allay his client's fears with flimsy hopes. From the beginning of their relationship, he made it clear that the prosecution would decline an invitation for a plea bargain.

Simons arrived about 11 am on the morning of November 30 to find Williams waiting at the south terminal of the Vancouver International Airport. The two drove back to Simons' office at 40 Powell Street in Vancouver where Simons reviewed Williams' new idea and explained that he held a few cards of his own, which he intended to play, but in the end, he would spend the greater portion of his court time refuting or casting reasonable doubt on the aspersions of the prosecution's many witnesses. To that point, Simons had been creating a detailed list of what-ifs. He had laid out every plausible angle the prosecutor could use and designed at least two alternatives in which he could put a positive spin on the outcome. As the case wore on, it was his intention to emphasize the events in the investigation that clearly indicated entrapment and abuse of process. With this approach, he felt confident the verdict would go in his client's favor.

By 9 p.m., Williams and Simons had shared all they could for the time being. It had been a long day, and Simons found it not always easy to keep his client focused on the legal proposition. Simons recounts, "Art tended to jump from one thought to another, and more often than not he wanted me to flow with his arguments rather than with those I had confidence in." Simons had a clear impression that home was the only place Williams wanted to be, so he drove him back to the south terminal of the airport and parked within fifty feet of the plane. He watched his client walk across the tarmac, climb into the cockpit and start the engine, whereupon he headed home.

Sid had flown with Williams on a couple of occasions and considered himself familiar with his habits and his attitudes about flying. He never appeared to Simons to be a risk taker. "He was a non-drinker," Simons says. "While I found comfort in my Bloody Mary's, he never had a cocktail or any form of liquor while I was with him. Whenever I flew with him he was extremely careful and fastidious about making sure everything worked the way it should. He had flown over to see me in Vancouver many times and there was never an incident that I was told about."

Once settled in his plane, Williams picked up the handset to his radio and contacted Norman Daynor, the traffic controller on duty, who cleared him to taxi runway 08.

Once the plane was airborne, Daynor's involvement became a matter of working in concert with the tower by monitoring the little bleep or target on his Ministry of Transport monitor as Williams' plane moved over the wetlands to the west of the airport and swung southwest towards home.

Historically, at 9 p.m. you would find the commercial traffic refueling, loading or off-loading cargoes, but an abnormality of Vancouver International Airport is that there are seldom flights coming or going at that time. The approach lanes were generally void of activity. Other than the weather, Williams could not have chosen a better time of the day to make his exit. At that moment, he owned the horizon.

There was no radar or instrumentation at the Nanaimo/Cassidy airstrip to aid aviators on their approach, so Vancouver had the practice of maintaining contact until a pilot touched down on the west side of the Strait of Georgia twenty minutes later.

Shirley stated, "Art called me from Simons' car approximately five minutes before he took off. He didn't always call me on his return, but on this occasion, he was coming back after dark and asked me to send Ridge off to the airport to light the kerosene lamps along the runway. There were no fixed lights back then. If you wanted the sides of the runway lit, someone had to physically go out onto the runway and light up a series of pots filled with kerosene." With this message relayed, Williams proceeded with his plans.

The high-level clouds from the early afternoon had diminished to fog with light rain. At nine o'clock, Vancouver Airport reported a measured ceiling of 1,000 feet, with an overcast layer of cloud above that at 2,400 feet. They also indicated light rain and some fog with visibility of four miles. The temperature was plus six degrees and the wind came out of the east at six knots. In contrast, the meteorological station at Cassidy

Airport reported a ceiling of 1,500 feet, with light rain and fog leaving the visibility at one and a half miles, with no wind.

Vancouver's North Shore mountains resembled a blackened wall as they rose from the water's edge, leaving an impregnable boundary to the north and east of the city. Williams' VFR (Visual Flight Rules) flight plan had stated he intended to make his way to the Cassidy Airport using visual headings. He would follow the lay of the land as he identified each of the Gulf Islands and establish his final approach to the Vancouver Island airstrip after fixing a visual reckoning on the opposing hillsides. With the weather closing in, the fellows in the tower considered such a plan to be foolhardy.

Because most of his route was over open water, visual references were compromised, especially in inclement weather. At the time of his departure from Vancouver, the weather was reported as being marginal VFR. The cloud level was so low along the eastern coast of Vancouver Island that he was told there would be no possibility of making a visual reference of any kind on his descent toward the Cassidy airstrip.

Norman Daynor clearly heard Williams call the Vancouver radar to report that he was westbound to Nanaimo, leveling at 4,000 feet. Daynor clarified Williams' current position and reminded him that his directional transponder had not been turned on. Williams told Daynor he'd had that problem before, and within minutes, Daynor was receiving Williams' signal.

It was precisely at 9:15 p.m. that the trouble began. Daynor saw Williams make an unauthorized turn. When he radioed Williams, he was told the plane was experiencing ADF problems and was returning to the airport. At that point, Williams was at 2,500 feet. With the heavy clouds blocking any light from the moon, visual reference over the open water was all but impossible. According to Daynor, "This may have been the reason he was attempting to use his ADF, which is an instrument in the plane designed as a navigational aid. He may have attempted to use a little bit of the ADF plus visual to make his way home. If indeed his ADF failed, he would have had no choice but to return to Vancouver." Daynor watched Williams' right turn getting tighter and tighter until it became a stationary dot on the radar, causing Daynor to radio Williams again to ask how he was making out. Twenty seconds later, Williams replied "I'm out of control," and all Daynor could do was watch the Cessna's blip vanish from his screen.

Aerial view of Cassidy (Nanaimo) airport
Credit: Web stock image

Don Bohun, Dale Elliott, Sid Simons 2008
Credit: Daryl Ashby

CHAPTER 19:

VANISHED

"Drug Apostle Vanishes in Georgia Strait"

—Lee King, Victoria Times Colonist

The crash investigator for the Ministry of Transport acknowledged at the enquiry that Williams had completed his night instrumentation training plus the training required for multi-engine endorsement, but the ministry had not received his request for a formal license endorsement. He had already used the training during his flight to Belize, and with his suggested military history, such an endorsement by Ministry of Transport officials might have been a mere formality.

Ministry of Transport officials concluded that Williams' plane had crashed just off the mouth of the Fraser River, seven miles west of the area known as the Sandheads, in approximately 1,200 feet of water, at 21:29 (9:29 p.m.), November 30, 1977.

Shirley Ferguson still recalls that night with a deep sense of loss. "I had sent Ray Ridge to the Cassidy Airport to light up the flares. A half hour went by and Ridge shows up at my door telling me that Art never showed up. I just told him to get himself back down there because

Art would be along shortly. We found out about the accident when the Vancouver Airport called my home and asked where Art's plane was. I told them he was flying in from Vancouver. After I hung up, I felt kind of funny, so I phoned the local radio station, thinking they may have had some news, and they told me that Art had crashed. It was a strange thing because two hours before I got the call from the Vancouver Airport, all the geese, ducks and dogs on our property went nuts. The geese were making this appalling noise, and the dogs were howling as if they knew what was about to happen."

Ruth Dashwood called Margaret shortly after and recalls that "Margaret was beside herself. When I suggested that he may have flown out of the area, she replied 'You don't know what you're talking about. Of course, he went down.'" Ruth said, Margaret was almost hysterical, and she definitely didn't want to consider the possibility that he had escaped.

Within minutes of the Vancouver Airport tower receiving the message that Williams' plane had gone down, staff contacted the Coast Guard hovercraft stationed at the Vancouver waterfront and asked the crew to check the site as soon as possible. Daynor put a grease spot on his monitor to pinpoint the geographical reference for later.

The hovercraft under Nigel Church left the Pacific Rescue Centre at precisely 9:37 p.m. on November 30, 1977. The subject of their search was a white with orange Cessna Hawk XP, model 172M, holding registration C-GIWQ, and showing ownership to Inkster Aircraft Corp. of Ladysmith B.C. They arrived at the crash site at 10 p.m. Twenty minutes later they spotted an aircraft seat and some other debris and launched a flashing strobe light to mark the position as the currents moved northwest. At 10:42 p.m. the U.S. Coast Guard Rescue helicopter advised Church that they were proceeding to join the search and in turn arrived at 10:50 p.m., whereupon they started dropping white flares to light up the scene.

The RCMP vessel *McClellan*, stationed at Steveston Harbor, joined them as well at 11:10 p.m. under the command of Cpl. William Frederick Gardner. At 1:30 a.m. the search received further help from the Coast Guard cutter, *Rider* plus the U.S. Navy destroyer *William H. Stanley*, which had been on exercises in the area. The three vessels searched two miles north and south of the crash site. At 1:40 a.m. they were joined by the Canadian armed forces Rescue Buffalo, which began dropping flares as well. Visibility was somewhat good. The Seaspan tug *Master* passed through the area with a couple of barges in tow and was told to scan the area with its searchlights as it continued, but it found nothing.

At 12:15 a.m. Church's hovercraft picked up an aircraft log book and some more debris, and fifteen minutes later they came alongside the patrol vessel *MP22* which had recovered a second log book as well as debris, all of which they took aboard the hovercraft. At 12:40 a.m. the hovercraft tied up to the *Rider* and took on board additional debris that they had collected. "The entirety of what we had in our possession included an aircraft seat which was badly bent, one broken sun visor, a white chalk commonly used to block an aircraft wheel, numerous pieces of paper, one of which was a fuel bill with Mr. Williams' name on it," Church recalls. "There was quite a lot of what we took to be cabin insulation from a light plane, a small first-aid kit and the two logbooks that were later identified as coming from IWQ, plus various cigarette packets and a rubber glove, which may or may not have been from the airplane."

At 4:30 a.m. the search disbanded because the wind was getting up, the seas were rising and they felt that further visual search wasn't doing any good. At 9:07 a.m. the search resumed to the west of the reported crash site along the eastern shores of Galiano and Valdes Islands. The searchers felt that the drift they had monitored on their strobe light could have possibly continued towards the islands with the wind. With that in mind, they searched from Salamanca Point up toward the north end of Gabriola Island. They searched the beaches and two miles offshore at quarter-mile spacing but found nothing. At the same time, the *Racer* continued to search the area in which they had placed the strobe. Church and his crew returned to the Rescue Centre at 10:33 a.m. Their search was resumed at 1:30 that afternoon with a different crew. Church stated, "The entirety of the search was intensive and focused on an area nineteen miles southwest of Vancouver, from a point seven degrees southwest of the Sandheads to the area immediately west of Robert's Bank."

On December 2nd, a spokesman for the Pacific Rescue Centre in Victoria announced that the search had been called off, and that the incident would be treated as a missing person's case by the RCMP. On December 26, 1977, the authorities reported finding a wheel, serial number GT5264, belonging to a small Cessna, attached to an undercarriage leg, serial number 774090, washed up on the shores near Little Campbell River, a short distance south of the crash site and thirty-five kilometers as the crow flies from Vancouver. The Canadian Coast Guard had predicted that if something had been missed during their search, currents in the Strait of Georgia would carry it to that point. The wheel showed signs of impact, with several cracks around the rim.

Although the Ladysmith property was in her name, Margaret was anxious to bring a settlement to what remained of her husband's estate. In the closing days of 1977 she applied to the courts for a declaration of her husband's death so that his will could be probated.

On March 5, 1978, Margaret attended the formal inquest into her husband's death, chaired by the coroner Dr. R.C. Talmey.

Sylvester Zeus, the aircraft accident investigator for the Ministry of Transport, testified that he had verified the serial number of the wheel retrieved was one off Williams' plane. In contrast, Charles Chambers of Cessna's head office in Wichita, Kansas, states, "Cessna places no serial numbers on its wheels or struts. There may have been a part number, but there is no way of correlating such a number back to a particular aircraft."

June Harrison, who had sold Art Williams the plane and who had done much of the work on it for Williams, commented, "I saw the wheel that the RCMP had recovered and it was not bent nor torn. There were no bent screws in the holes as though it was torn away from the carriage and absolutely no physical evidence of damage or rust for that matter."

Happy Laffin recalls being at Williams' home the day after his disappearance. "I was collecting a few personal tools that I had left there, when a friend of Art's by the name of Frank Warder showed up, so I asked him what he was up to. He stated he had come over to collect the strut and wheel that he had loaned Art."

Williams had made numerous trips over to Hudson Island, which is located three miles north of Chemainus in Stuart Channel and just west of Thetis Island to have tea with the elderly resident. The island had a rough grass strip that proved a challenge to anyone not seasoned, but Laffin suggested, Williams had landed hard a month or two prior to his disappearance and bent the strut or leg on his plane. To keep him airborne, Frank loaned him a spare assembly that he had lying about. No one can verify whether Williams had repaired his wheel and strut, leaving doubt that the one Williams had affixed to his plane the night of November 30 was the original.

As for the seat that was recovered, it was originally thought to be the pilot's seat on the left until investigators were told that Williams had replaced his seat shortly after purchasing the plane with an articulating one. It not only moved front to back, but, because he had difficulty seeing over the instrument panel, it moved up and down as well. Don Bohun mentioned, Williams had retained the original seat for posterity.

Shirley adds, "Art was having problems with his gauges, so he flew it down to Victoria on November 27 for the regulated hundred-hour inspection. He got it back fully certified air worthy on the morning he crashed."

One of the inquest jurors asked the meteorologist, Tom Gigliotti, if Williams' carburetor could have suffered from icing. Gigliotti responded, "Freezing level was estimated at 3,500 feet so there may have been a chance." But Don Bohun was attending the inquest and pointed out that the engine in Williams' Cessna was fuel-injected and therefore not subject to icing. A juror asked Church, "Should there have been an oil slick in those sea conditions?" Church answered, "Yes."

A member of the jury asked if Williams was considered skilled enough to fly in the weather conditions of that night. The representative for the Ministry of Transport stated, "I have no personal knowledge of Mr. Williams' flying ability, but personally I believe anybody flying with visual flight only, would be able to navigate quite easily."

The crash investigator noted that Art's personal flight log indicated that he had flown "over 951 hours between September 7, 1977, and November 27, 1977," equating to more than ten hours per day, without a day of rest. The Ministry of Transport's records, however, show he only registered the required pre-flight plans for a total of 300 hours during that time. With Williams' habit of not filing flight plans, the difference came as no surprise. What was surprising was the fact that there are few if any commercial pilots who log those kinds of hours.

After all the evidence was given, the jury found that "Arthur James Williams died in or near the Strait of Georgia, British Columbia, due to a plane crash, resulting from a lack of night flying experience and the cause of death was drowning."

Having spent millions of dollars on bringing Williams to court, the police were reluctant to close their books without some conclusive evidence that Williams' plane had indeed sunk in the deepest part of the inland ocean. A request had been made to send the scientific research sub Pisces down in the 200 fathoms of water to scour the ocean floor. Had they found the plane, the only question remaining would have been 'Was Williams still strapped into the left-hand seat of the cockpit?'

In the end the Canadian government concluded that it had spent far too much already on the case, and the $20,000 price for the Pisces expedition would be throwing good money after bad.

On December 2, 1977, the exploits of Art Williams finally made the front page of all the dailies. The Victoria Colonist, a paper that had been in circulation since 1858, ran an article by Lee King titled "Drug Apostle Vanishes in Georgia Strait." During his life, Williams was relegated to the second page; yet his death garnered headlines fitting his notoriety.

But was he dead? In the thirty-one minutes that elapsed between the moment Williams' plane vanished from Daynor's monitor to the time that the hovercraft arrived at the site, could Williams have carried out an elaborate disappearing act? Did the Cessna, with its cruising speed of 131 knots or 150 miles per hour, carry him well clear of Canadian air space by the time the posse arrived?

CHAPTER 20:

DEAD OR ALIVE?

If he were still alive, he would be thumbing his nose at the authorities much like Hannibal Lector.

—Constable Jerry Moloci

Lee King, journalist for The Times Colonist wrote: "Was Williams really a victim of the crash or was it all an elaborate plan to escape. Opinions from those who were involved in his life differ as widely as the personalities themselves."

To add credence to the theory that Art perished, the control center for the Vancouver Airport reported that it failed to pick up signals from any boats or other airplanes in the vicinity at the time of the crash. That statement suggests that the airport's radar could in fact isolate a small pleasure craft the size of a skiff or runabout moving across the surface of the water. On the other hand, when pressed on the matter during the accident inquest, Norman Daynor confessed, "Below a hundred feet, we probably wouldn't have him on prime radar."

It was further revealed that the Vancouver radar of the day was unable to determine the elevation of the aircraft without the pilot physically telling them what it was. Part of the RCMP transcript of conversations between Williams and their informant E752 in the months preceding the disappearance, records an intriguing exchange that poses an interesting question. In this conversation, E752 says, "I've discovered something really nice. I flew from Seattle with this other guy up to Cassidy, didn't report to nobody, just came right in at forty-five hundred feet, landed in Nanaimo and tied up to your spot. It was an American plane and we hitchhiked into town, picked up my sample, whipped back to the plane and flew back down to the Boeing Field, threw some gas in it and flew back over to that little place I showed you. I didn't report to anybody and at no time did anybody ever come on us. We just used an intermittent transponder."

Williams' response to this was, "Don't even turn the transponder on! In the States, they don't even care about anything that's below five thousand feet. They will pick you up if you have the transponder on. If you descend out of the radar they don't concern themselves. You can fly along at seven hundred feet; you can go anywhere, and they don't care."

Donald Bohun, Williams' lawyer and trusted friend, believes Art was killed in the crash yet he still wonders how Williams could outmaneuver the Cubans, as he had done during the aborted trip to Belize only a matter of months before his disappearance, yet succumb to typical West Coast elements. Bohun punctuates this thought with the comment, "Art did ask me for a list of countries where Canada had no extradition rights prior to his disappearance and Belize was on that list. When we were in Belize, Art did get to know a lot of people who would hide him."

Williams made numerous trips in his Cessna during the weeks that followed his preliminary hearing. There is no record of where he went or why. Speculation abounds that he took this time to prepare for his exit and shuffled millions of dollars in drug money to a safe-haven somewhere offshore. The story of choice suggests he is retired and living comfortably in the Caribbean, possibly on one of the Grand Cayman Islands or in Belize. Rumors have circulated that he had purchased land on the islands, which might explain the trip he made with Bohun in 1977. In addition, Williams had added wing tips, a larger propeller and secondary fuel tanks to his Cessna to increase its range and versatility. Such added expense could not have been justified for local jaunts.

Added to these rumors is a true story related by Dale Elliott. During the day, preceding Williams' disappearance, he and Art had discussed the idea of purchasing a large boat on the mainland and fleeing the heat along with Ridge, plus our respective families, to Belize. "We had all gone in mass to acquire our passports, and we were ready to run. Art told us most of the logistics were in place, but when he went missing the scheme vanished along with him. The day he disappeared, Arthur stated he had the money set aside to finance the plan, but I told him we would talk about it tomorrow."

Richard Jackson, the son of Williams' flying instructor, and a certified instructor is skeptical that Williams survived. Jackson knew first-hand the problems associated with the Cessna 172M. "The plane's vacuum pump which drives the altitude indicator, the instrument that tells how stable the plane is in flight, had a flaw. There were several reports of it breaking down. It happened at least once to Williams prior to November 30." Jackson insisted that it was not a fault of the audio direction finder that brought on Williams' demise, but rather the altitude indicator. As Jackson stressed, "Art never had sufficient training to fly by instruments, so he never would have recognized the situation at hand."

Jason Grist, a flight control instructor at the Vancouver Air Traffic Control Centre stated, "Unless you had instrumentation training, you would become totally disoriented if you lost your visual reference with the ground beneath you. You get what they call vertigo, where you lose all sense of direction. You could be in a steep spiral with a crash as the only outcome, yet your inner senses tell you that you are flying straight and level."

Jackson feels there is a high likelihood that vertigo is exactly what happened to Art Williams. In his words, "He was in a death trap spiral with no escape. He would have hit the water with a force greater than 1,400 pounds per square inch, enough pressure to snap the seat buckle like a piece of yarn. Enough force to hurtle the seat and Williams through the windshield. The plane would have been demolished on impact."

If that was the case, one would have to question where was all the wreckage that should have been scattered over the surface of the water. There has never been a crash where some fragment of wing or tail isn't left floating on the surface and, as reported at the inquest, there was no oil residue from the near full tank of fuel and engine lubricant.

A high-level officer in the armed forces went on record as saying, "There was nothing within the debris that was found that would support the theory of a crash. Everything inclusive of the seat, piece of carpet, log books, tire block and scraps of insulation could easily have been jettisoned from the plane as it maintained the circle witnessed by the air traffic controller."

Though the RCMP have officially closed the book on Art Williams' case, individual members of the force are confident that he is alive. Off the record, members point toward his expertise as a pilot and his reported participation in a Second World War glider assault against the City of Arnhem, Netherlands. Others support their opinion by stating that he was trained as a parachutist and practiced many low-level jumps during those war years. Still others within the force, who prefer to remain anonymous, feel that as an intellectual who despised authority in every guise, he most certainly would have masterminded the ultimate escape and staged his own death. "He had everything to gain." He was facing a trial and if convicted would be spending the better part of his remaining years behind bars.

Ken Sutherland, the former chief of the Ladysmith RCMP detachment, knew Williams since the early 1960s and shares the popular point of view. "Not for a minute do I think he is dead. Knowing Art and having dealt with him for so many years, I'm sure he set it all up. Art had a hell of a mind. It just happened to be headed in the wrong direction. Had he used it in a legal way, he could have done almost anything. Art had a chip on his shoulder towards the law and any form of bureaucracy. He barked a lot but rarely bit."

Sutherland is also skeptical about the wreckage that washed up on shore. "What they found of the aircraft was nothing that couldn't have been tossed out. Nothing from the plane was recovered that was integral to the structure. There wasn't anything found that would indicate a plane crash." A top-ranking officer in the armed forces suggested that had he known there would have been such limited evidence of a plane in trouble, he'd never even have ordered a search. "Williams could easily have faked the messages heard by the control tower. That would be Art Williams; he was capable of doing that."

Al Hickman, the Saanich municipal constable who was brought in to do some of the investigation's controversial work, holds the same opinion. He worked on the case for four years and feels he knew Williams as well as anyone on the force. "Why did he fly at the altitude he did? Ministry of Transport tapes record Williams saying at takeoff that he would be flying at 1,000 feet. Then, after he had developed problems and was fighting to control his plane, he told the air controller his altitude was 2,500 feet. Art hated flying at night. Why would he go to such a height if it weren't to parachute out? He knew he was going down for a lot of years. He was looking at the end of the world as he knew it and he knew the tax man was going to do a number on him. There is no doubt the guy was an intellectual genius. In intellect, he was obviously a giant, not just in MDA but so many other things. He was a most amazing guy and that's the reason I don't believe he's dead." And there's further proof that they believe Art didn't die.

Apparently, Art often talked about Lou Brown and how Lou had gone to the west coast of New Zealand where he started a prawn-fishing business. Williams had expressed an interest in going there and doing that as well. According to Lou Brown, "Not long after Art disappeared, four cops, two Canadian and two New Zealanders, turned up at our remote home, only to find Art wasn't there. Would the authorities have gone to that trouble if they didn't believe they could find him?"

Art's family and closest of friends are also of two minds about the accident: was it staged so Art could get away or did Art die?

Ruth Loomis thinks that Art flew a few feet off the water to Hudson Island just west of Thetis and Kuper Islands and from there caught a ride to friendlier soil. Ruth said, Art took Margaret there on one occasion and it was nothing more than a grass strip, 1,900 feet in length, with a significant rise in elevation towards the south. It was full of potholes and had a dog's leg that hooked to the left about two-thirds of the way along. It was not a landing strip for amateurs or those who were faint of heart. But, as Ruth says, "By the time Art disappeared, he had developed quite a relationship with the old hermit who lived in a small cabin on the island and would fly in just for tea and biscuits."

For her part, Margaret supported the theory that her estranged husband died in the crash.

Art's common-law wife Shirley Ferguson also believes Art died. She said, "After all that I have gone through since November 30, 1977, if he did show up, he probably wouldn't live long after I was finished with him." But would Art have deliberately walked away from his family and friends?

Kristine Loomis has an interesting take on that. She says, "Art always spoke of people who tried to escape their surroundings, and Art would say, 'The primary mistake that they made was their inability to separate themselves from their emotional attachment to friends and family.' He saw it as a weakness."

With this psychology and pending years of incarceration, Art Williams had the motivation to stage his disappearance. But again, the question remains: could he physically pull it off? Perhaps a story from Shirley's young son, Terry sheds light on the matter.

His step dad had definitely graduated beyond the level of a novice flier. "There was one occasion when Lou Brown and I were with Dad and he wanted to see if his Cessna could do a loop, an act which the manufacturers cautioned against. He proceeded to take that thing into a vertical climb until it just died out and started plummeting downward. The ground was coming up fast and Art was pulling for all he was worth on the wheel. As he had predicted, that little plane came out of the dive so he proceeded to take it through a second loop, which caused it to conk out. We found out later that when the plane was inverted, the fuel would drain from the tanks and it simply ran out of fuel. Art had no choice but to make an emergency landing in a farmer's field. He never got the least bit flustered but used the farmer's phone to call one of his friends, who brought us ten gallons of fuel so we could get back to the Cassidy Airport.

"When it came to flying, nothing much stopped him from doing what he wanted to do. Even before he completed the necessary courses for his instrumentation certification, he used to fly all the time at night. In his own words, 'who in hell is going to tell me that I can't fly in the dark?'"

Allen Dashwood supports Terry Ferguson's position. About his uncle's ability as a pilot, he says. "I flew with him a few times, and as for his talents as a pilot, they were pretty impressive. He didn't need an airport to set down. If he saw an open field or just a level stretch of land, he would put his Cessna down on a dime and give you change, just for the thrill of proving he could do it or because someone said he couldn't. He didn't always have a reason for what he did, sometimes just because it was a challenge was reason enough."

Stanley Cross had a chance to listen to the tape of Williams' distress call on that fateful evening. "Art loved theatrics. Often, he would fly into this rage just to scare the hell out of someone, and on those occasions when we were together, he would turn towards me just enough for me to catch a wink out of the corner of his eye. Those tapes held the same theatrical voice that I was familiar with. There is no way he was out of control the night he disappeared. He knew exactly what he was doing. I had predicted his disappearance for years, and when I heard the tape I just laughed. I knew the scenario would end with Art flying back from Vancouver, it would be late at night and the purported loss would be in the deepest water lying between Vancouver and the Cassidy Airport."

Art's long-time friend Hap Laffin has information that might confirm Cross' theory. A few days before he disappeared, Williams asked Hap which inlet along the BC Lower Mainland held the deepest water? He knew that Laffin had fished up and down the coast and would know the answer.

Constable Jerry Moloci believes Williams is dead just based on the man's personality. "He had such a pent-up anger for authority," Moloci says, "that he would call us Gestapo every time we met, which I'm sure reflects his hatred for the Nazis of the Second World War. Had he applied all that energy to good means, he would have done very well in life. He was a brilliant man with an incredible amount of knowledge in most everything. If he were still alive, he would be thumbing his nose at the authorities much like Hannibal Lector."

CHAPTER 21:

WHO'S ON TRIAL?

The fact remains, the RCMP were the ones on trial. At best, when it comes to Art, I left them with mitigating damage.

—E752

Robbed of their ultimate victory when Williams vanished, the authorities turned their attention toward his associates. The trial of Ray Ridge, the only defendant in custody, began in the first week of October 1978. Even though he was the least of the three players, a guilty verdict would pave the way for a solid conviction for Dale Elliott at such a time he was apprehended, and Williams, if his disappearance turned out to be some elaborate hoax.

On opening day, the courtroom was so quiet; a simple thought would have created an echo. The prosecution once again took the form of Branson and Taylor, who felt confident everything had been planned to perfection. They had employed experts in every field to prepare their case so there would be no loose ends. The only thing they could not prepare for was what their bad-boy witness E752 was going to offer in the way of a testimony. From speaking with Chester Kary, they knew that there was no way they were going to corral his comments into something predictable.

James D. Taylor took the floor and led several RCMP through their involvement in the case and their personal knowledge of each piece of evidence. By October 30, 1978, Taylor had finished up by walking Staff Sgt. George Eppy through all the standing evidence. Eppy was the identification expert for the RCMP, and the Crown relied heavily on his proficiency to establish a solid foundation upon which to build their case.

When it was his turn, Simons came out of the chute looking for some white-collar blood. With a fist-full of notes, he did his best to bring Eppy to his knees. Simons' strategy was to peel back the layers of lies, half-truths and careless preparation from the testimony of all the Crown witnesses. His first goal was to unravel Eppy's evidence. Staff Sgt. George Eppy insisted on using his own drawings to give evidence about the layout of the secret lab, but he was unable to satisfy Simons as to where it was situated within the overall structure. Simons pressed him as to why he didn't pay the municipal hall a visit to gain a copy of Williams' building plans. Eppy insisted that he "was accustomed to relying upon his own expertise in drafting." Simons wanted to know if he had confirmed that the building in question was in fact on Williams' land and not part of the neighboring property. Eppy's response was "no." Had he or any of his peers "lifted fingerprints from anything or from any place within Williams' so-called secret lab to validate the presence of the accused or his peers?" His answer again was a resounding "no." When Simons asked the witness about the photographic evidence he had taken, Eppy had to admit that a few items in the photos had been moved from their original location by the officers who had gained access to the area before Eppy and therefore the photographic evidence stood compromised before the court.

In Simons' opinion, Eppy had failed miserably to substantiate any evidence worthy of the court's consideration. He appeared to be not as diligent as he could have been, and the evidence pointed clearly to the possibility that Eppy had not put his whole heart and soul into his work. If that were the case, there was ample room to cast reasonable doubt.

When the Crown's star witness, E752 took the stand on November 22nd, Branson questioned him. He led him back to his initial introduction to Williams and how Don Bohun had been instrumental in making that happen. Attempting to rattle Branson, Simons interrupted his delivery again and again asking for this and clarification of that to be reorganized or deleted from the records for any number of reasons. Judge Millward became so unsettled by the constant barrage that he admonished Simons, "You are too impatient and you had better take it a little easier. We'll get there much quicker if you do."

E752 told the court that he had acquired what he believed to be 140 ounces of MDA from a fellow in Vancouver named Chilton Durango, and he wanted Williams to confirm that it was bona fide. He stated that he spoke with Bohun and asked if he knew of someone who could analyze it for him. Bohun recommended that he take it to a company in Vancouver that did that sort of thing. This was not what E752 wanted to hear, so he went directly to Williams and asked for his help. In time, he received a verbal report via Bohun stating that it was not MDA but rather some form of speed, at which point E752 returned to Vancouver, where he sold it to someone who was dealing in that area of the market.

As the Crown finished its examination, Simons went to work portraying their principal witness as a psychotic who was capable of just about anything, including concocting an elaborate story about Williams, Elliott and Ridge for the sole purpose of covering over his own illicit activities.

Within the first few questions of his cross-examination, however, Simons realized he was facing an uphill grind at getting a straight answer out of the witness. His opening question, "Where were you born?" earned a snide reply, "Are you talking to me?" His second question didn't go much better. "What's your education?" All he got back was "Very minimal." Feeling the temperature rising beneath his starched collar,

Simons tossed back, "That doesn't help us much," to which the witness added, "That's right, it didn't help me much either."

Fearful that his session was going to turn into some sort of vaudeville act, Simons tore into the informant's testimony like a rabid dog, ripping away at any opening he could find. His primary goal was to undermine his evidence and leave him floundering before the court as a witness without credibility. Simons called him a liar and had him confess to the court that lying was what he did best to gain the trust of the defendants. Simons asked the court how it could rely so heavily on his testimony when it was clear that telling the truth was not part of his makeup.

Amazingly enough, throughout the entire attack, the informant never once lost his cool. If anything, his responses were geared to taunt his accuser to a point of apoplexy. He not only managed to keep his story intact, but in the battle with his accuser, he gave back just about as good as he got. Simons chose to revisit the testimony regarding E752's having Williams test the substance he had purchased on the mainland in hopes of verifying it as being MDA. Simons asked, "Were you not told [by Williams] that it was the kind of thing you should flush down the toilet?"

E752 replied, "Well something that gets flushed down the toilet is something that is a personal opinion. There are things Mr. Williams might flush down the toilet that I may put up my nose or into my stomach. I was concerned with what I put on the street so far as it was what it was labeled to be."

Simons tried to unnerve him. "But you sold it to the person who put it out ultimately as what?"

"As MDA."

"And you went along with it?"

"Why shouldn't I?"

"If it was arsenic and you found that out, would you sell it to someone to sell as MDA?"

"Don't be ridiculous. I took enough care to find out what it was I was selling before I sold it. I am not making a moral distinction. I am making a scientific distinction. It is money received from goods provided. It is a business proposition."

Simons demanded to know why he had acquired chemical beakers and other glassware from Williams, which had not been brought before the court as evidence. Without hesitation, the witness replied that he wanted them to test the quality of the cocaine he was importing from Colorado. Under oath he confessed that he was involved in far more than the distribution of Williams' MDA, but this only caused Simons to stress for the benefit of the court, that his client, Raymond Ridge, was a choir boy compared to the Crown's key witness.

Simons asked E752 if he had ever given marijuana to Corporal Chester Kary, to which the witness replied that he had. When pressed, he stated he gave him a sample of what he was currently selling on the streets; at that time, he had hundreds of pounds of the product in his keeping. Simons pushed on, "Did you give him any cocaine?" He replied, "Yes. Within the last six months I gave him two to three hundred milligrams of what I brought in from Colorado."

Simons inquired why the Attorney General would authorize such a costly investigation into a crime that would warrant a maximum sentence of ten years when, to its full knowledge, the key witness was importing contraband that would gain him a life sentence.

Simons drove the informant into a corner where he had no choice but to admit that Kary knew he was carrying cocaine either in his clothing or his car during those times the officer searched his person and vehicle. "In fact," E752 stated, "I had offered a taste to Kary on numerous occasions, with him brushing it aside. I offered him some Thai weed that I had brought in, suggesting it would cure a headache he had at the time, but he never took me up on it."

The informant also admitted under oath that he had carried a loaded .38 Smith & Wesson in addition to a .25 caliber semi-automatic revolver on the many occasions that Kary had searched him and his vehicle. In his own words, he testified that Kary had seen the .38 in his glove box and all he did was admonish him on the possibility that he "would get hurt by carrying them." His response, "Everyone who matters knows I carried them, so that in itself garners me the respect that I need; as yet, it has never become a necessity to use them. You might say they are my insurance policy."

Simons attempted to drive home again and again the disservice to the public when Kary allowed the witness to keep the MDA that had been purchased with public funds and, in turn, allowed him to garner a healthy profit from its resale. The result was that the question remained: was E752 an RCMP mole in Williams' organization or was he one of Williams' moles in the RCMP inner workings?

As the informant later said, "They were trying to put a circle around Art, but I was taping the RCMP as much as I was taping Art. The fact remains, the RCMP were the ones on trial; the hunter was the hunted. At best, when it comes to Art, I left them with mitigating damage."

Simons wove his attack in such a way that the Crown's informant told the court how his "flying lessons had been paid for by the RCMP through the liberal generosity of Corporal Kary." Kary confirmed, "The RCMP paid for his flying license because we thought it would add a connection to Art's interests."

The informant explained that he "purchased a Beechcraft Bonanza airplane from the proceeds of his drug sales" and that Kary knew of his solo flights outside the three-mile zone to which learners were restricted. He also explained that he was "travelling to the United States to bring back over a ton of marijuana and far too many pounds of cocaine to remember"; he did this even after he had failed to complete the final examination for his official flying license. "I would come and go from the States with no serious interdiction. I would just use uncontrolled airports, logging camps and the likes. I never kept a flight log, as required by the Ministry of Transport, because it was just too much trouble to do so. On occasion, I would rent a Cessna from Victoria Flying Services' office in Nanaimo or a Cardinal aircraft from Willard Flying Services at Payne Field in Seattle, using the name Randy Blankenship just to mix things up."

He elaborated, "Art developed this attitude wherein he made it known that you don't call him, he'll call you and only when he's good and ready. If he wouldn't cooperate with me, I would dive bomb his house to get his attention. I'd start at 7,000 feet, shut the motor off, and then pull out again just over the top of his house while firing the motor back up. The racket from the engine under full power only a hundred or so feet above his roof would thunder through the thin walls of his house and scare the hell out of him. It rattled him so much that he would come out shaking his fists at me, but I got his attention. When I met up with him later he would yell at me, 'Don't you know that is illegal,' to which I would reply, 'and so is what you are doing, so what is your point?'"

Kary explained, "We didn't really monitor his [E752] movements other than when he was involved with Art. We only had five or six guys at the time, which always left us short of resources."

Intelligence gathering was still a gentleman's game where we were left having to place an ear to a keyhole, rely on physical observation or manually eavesdrop on a suspect's telephone conversation. Unlike today where technology allows us to scan a million independent conversations in a millisecond looking for key words; manpower then was a primary prerequisite, a commodity in short supply.

E752 proceeded to outline how he had crashed his new plane on Hudson Island while trying to find an alternate location to off-load marijuana that he was importing from the US and how, at the time, he had three passengers on board, all of whom had been drinking and were high on weed. He explained that he had abandoned the plane rather than report the injuries associated with the crash, which would certainly cause him to lose the right to fly. E752 explained that when the Ministry of Transport put pressure on the RCMP to investigate the matter, Kary eventually completed the report on his behalf and encouraged the feds to push the matter aside. To E752, this was a mere inconvenience that he simply couldn't find the time for in his busy life.

E752's friend Dewy Babcock was on board at the time of the crash and his memory of the incident is different. "Contrary to the report, it was more of a joyride than anything as sinister as what the courts have recorded. His Beechcraft was just too fast a plane for landing on such a rough strip. When we touched down, one of our wheels hung up in a pothole, which spun the plane into the trees. This tore the first wing off, and then we swung the other way and tore off the second wing. That turned out to be a good thing because the wings held all the fuel, hence there was no risk of fire. The fuselage, with him, me, and the two girls in it, bounced along through the trees until it came to a stop and we all leapt out. The front seat tore loose and came back on my ankles, leaving them cut and bleeding. Otherwise we were in pretty good shape. No question about it, we were all high. We had been smoking Thai Sticks and drinking Grand Marnier. Fortunately for us, there was a guy fishing in the waters nearby. Seeing us go down, he made straight for the island. By that time, we had cleaned up what we didn't want anybody to see and stumbled out to the clearing, as the guy was running up the airstrip towards us. We threw our arms around him, jumped into his boat and wasted no time making our way over to the Chemainus wharf. I flipped a taxi driver fifty bucks to forget he saw us, and we caught a ride back to our vehicle at the Cassidy Airport."

According to Elliott, it was Dewy Babcock who connected E752 to everyone in the Pacific Northwest who mattered. The two of them had freighted over a ton of marijuana from Vashon Island in Puget Sound into Victoria's Inner Harbor. E752 recalls, "To set the record straight, I never did any deals with Dewy." He continued, "During one run I was having problems with the boat's motor and had to tie up to the public docks in Victoria's Inner Harbor in front of the Empress Hotel. It sat there for three days before I could get the motor running again, and by the second day you could smell that weed a block away. I will never know why the cops didn't step in and scoop up the load. There is no way they didn't know it was there."

The informant told the court that he had purchased an inflatable boat, plus an eighteen-foot inboard / outboard, and on numerous occasions used them to import hundreds of pounds of marijuana. The defense outlined to the court how the mole had ripped off three Americans for $35,000 by not paying for a quantity of marijuana that he imported into Canada. When the three came gunning, Kary tucked him away in a safe house and negotiated with the US Drug Enforcement Agency to pick the three up on a variety of charges.

In exchange for services rendered, E752 agreed to assist the DEA when his Canadian handlers cut him loose, but according to him, "The report that I ripped off the Americans is not true. I wouldn't drop a dime on those guys. I was just late in paying. There was no DEA involved unless they were brought in by the RCMP unknown to me. Those guys were ex-Viet Nam and they weren't the type you'd forego paying. They would have sooner scalped me than look at me. They ended up paying me a visit and I told them that this other guy owed me money and another guy owed me money. They just looked those fellows up and collected from them. Following that they took their money back across the border and reinvested it."

The RCMP's mole continued to beguile the court by telling them that his sole purpose in helping the RCMP was to eliminate his competition, then take over their turf and profit by increasing his market share of the industry. He asked nothing from the RCMP save his expenses, and in his opinion they had agreed to turn a blind eye to his illicit activities. The only formal concession they agreed on was to "protect my next of kin from any possible repercussions." When asked by Simons what that meant, he replied, "You can't send people to jail and not expect recrimination from the underworld. Repercussions could range from a black eye to a funeral service."

Simons asked, "Is that why you were carrying a loaded .25 caliber automatic?"

"Yes," was his reply.

"The fact is," says E752, "I feared Art Williams more than anyone else in my life at that time. I fully expected something to come down in that courtroom during the bail hearing or after in the form of a sniper. I was packing and ready to defend myself.

One day Sid Simons came forward and asked the informant, "Are you presently standing here in court with a restricted firearm on your person?'

The informant turned and caught the eye of the Crown Counsel, who immediately asked for a recess. Branson and Chester Kary hauled their witness into an anteroom and found two firearms in his belt. After they got over the shock, the two hid them between two large books in the room's library and went back into the courtroom, where their witness returned to the stand. When Simons asked the same question about carrying a gun, E752 replied, "Your Honor, as God is my witness, I am not packing a firearm."

For the duration of the trial, E752 was paid $600 per month as a living allowance. When the case files were closed, the RCMP agreed to provide him with a new identity and $75,000 toward his relocation. According to Kary, "At that time it was the largest award given." From that day forward, the informant would live by his personal motto "Those who look for me and find me make their own peril," which he believed was best relayed in Spanish: *"Los que me buscan y me encuentran lo hacen a su propio peligro."*

When the court allowed the informant's testimony to stand as evidence against Ray Ridge, Simons stood shaking his head in disbelief.

In retrospect, E752 came to feel, "I had been deceived from the beginning by those who were using me, leaving me ashamed for the part that I played. The motives they portrayed were in fact not their real motives. Art was my mentor and I was learning from him. He showed me how to make 82 percent cocaine hydrochloride. My dad taught me how to shoot and handle guns, but Art could tear down my automatic pistol and reassemble it in military time. Even so, he hated guns and would insist I unload them whenever I was at his place. The story about the MDA is a small part of the big picture. Art did far more good than bad. He was a war hero, a scientist, and a man who was just trying to make a living before his time. He would read the Fisher Scientific Catalogue like I would read Sears.

"Of all the RCMP I encountered, Bob Hawkes was the only one who I remember fondly. He was a good guy with good intentions. When I was first sucked into this case, he took me aside and told me to get the hell out of undercover life, take my wife and get out of Dodge, so to speak. Unfortunately, I didn't avail myself of his wisdom and proceeded in my usual badder than the guy they wanted to catch approach. I was an unmanageable commodity."

Sid Simons recalls, "I honestly felt that Kary had stepped over the line so many times that his vision of impropriety had become blurred. To my way of thinking, he was a man who identified with his informant and in some hideous way wanted to be him. To prove my point, I demanded that he open his shirt in court so that the judge and jury could see the gold-plated razor blade that hung around his neck. This symbol of the underworld was his substitute for a Saint Christopher medallion and, not unlike those he had taken an oath to incarcerate, the blade was a tool or instrument worn by cocaine users and demonstrated how his relationship with the informant had grown beyond mere supervision as a cop. With no way to retreat, he unbuttoned his shirt, but only after my insistence. As expected, it had the effect I believed it would on those who mattered most."

As the defense arguments drew to a close, Judge Peter Millward instructed the jury that they "had to consider all those who knew of or participated in the suspect's actions as co-conspirators, and for the benefit of the jury such an accusation should include Officer Kary and Crown Counsel Branson, plus their prized informant." According to Millward, the named men knowingly participated in the purchase and distribution of contraband and knew that in doing so they were in viola-tion of the law. Millward was clearly instructing the jury to assume the same level of guilt for those members of the RCMP who had attempted to bring Williams, Elliott and Ridge to justice as they would for E752 or Ridge. In essence, if the jury considered the RCMP officers blameless, they must in turn find the defendant not guilty. If, on the other hand, the defendant was considered guilty, it left the door open for charges to be brought against Kary, Branson and the informant, E752. In Judge Millward's eyes, all men were truly equal.

The hearings lasted just shy of one month, and at the end the jury convicted Raymond Albert Ridge on October 30 of conspiracy to traffic in MDA and three counts of trafficking MDA. This was not the first case involving MDA to hit the courts, but all the other cases involved the trafficking of much smaller amounts and only at a street level. This was the first conviction in the Pacific Northwest involving the manufacturer at the original point of supply. For services rendered, Ridge received an invoice from Sid Simons in the amount of $22,000.

On December 27, 1978, Ridge was sentenced to three years for conspiracy and one year concurrent for each of the trafficking charges. If anyone thought for one moment it would end there, they were dreadfully wrong. Before the ink had dried on the judge's summary, Simons had filed an appeal based on the argument that the county court judge's instructions to the jury were incomplete. Ridge won a temporary bid for freedom by posting a $20,000 appeal bond. The British Columbia Court of Appeal heard Simons' argument on July 23, 1979 and on December 7 upheld the trafficking convictions but acquitted him of the conspiracy charge. A mistrial was ordered leaving the decision for a new trial on the table.

The Attorney General felt too much money had already been spent bringing these renegades to justice, so the prosecutor was told to come to a settlement that would work for both the Crown and the defendant. It was agreed behind closed doors that Ridge would serve less than a year for the charges at hand.

Such sentences enrage the agencies that spend so much time attempting to suppress criminal activity, yet in Canada, sentences like this are the norm. In contrast, if the same individual were tried in an American court, he or she would literally rot in jail.

Sid Simons, who had become a member of the criminal justice section of the Canadian Bar Association, was not about to leave the issue as it rested in the courts. In February 1979, the McDonald Royal Commission met to investigate possible wrongdoings committed by members of the RCMP in the process of carrying out their duties. The commission was established in 1977 after it became public knowledge that the RCMP Security Service had been caught in illegal and improper activities.

The BC Civil Liberties Association was more specific in a document it presented to the commission, noting that the RCMP had been caught in the act of "breaking and entering into a legitimate news agency; secreting away, copying, and returning tapes containing membership lists of a legitimate political party; opening first class mail, burning down barns, gathering confidential medical information on suspects, and fomenting violence using forged letters." In reality, the RCMP had burned down a barn to prevent the meeting of a number of militant nationalists and American radicals; they broke into the offices of a Montreal left-wing news agency, stealing and destroying some of their files; and they broke into the Parti Quebecois headquarters and stole its membership lists.

On February 1, Simons submitted a paper to Mr. Justice David McDonald outlining what he considered to be criminal behavior on the part of an officer of the law.

Simons' statement: "These people [RCMP] are sworn to uphold the law and prevent the commission of offences and yet they are involved actively and creatively in the commission of offences." Simons stated that his client's conviction rested on the testimony of a paid RCMP informer regarding activities between May 1976 and August 1977. "During the course of that period he [E752] imported into Canada and trafficked two tons of marijuana, several pounds of cocaine and he also trafficked in speed. In addition, the informer brought two unregistered handguns into Canada and filed a false report after crashing a plane, carrying passengers while flying with an inadequate license. So is it so important, that they convict Williams and Ridge that they let a guy traffic two tons of marijuana and cocaine and commit numerous other offences while putting people in jeopardy. He gets a license to deal with impunity and puts the finger on other people."

The informant, stated Simons would even traffic the MDA he purchased from Williams and Ridge with taxpayer money, and he estimated the informant made $2.5 million as a result of the concessions granted by the RCMP, yet had never been charged for any of the related offences. Cpl. Chester Kary of the RCMP was the officer commissioned to handle the informant. Kary responded within the trial transcript, "As far as I was concerned, he was going to traffic that whether he worked for me or not, and effectively by working for me, that traffic was going to cease as soon as Williams' investigation was over."

Jan O'Brien of the Vancouver Express reported that at the time of Simons' submission, Justice McDonald "denied him the opportunity because he failed to present a written brief to the commission prior to its two-day public hearing in Vancouver." Simons wondered how a public body commissioned to seek justice could turn a blind eye to something so criminal when it was delivered to them on a silver platter. To the lay person, it smacked of another government-sponsored study designed to fabricate an illusion of justice. Simons stated, "While the informant was gathering evidence, he committed about forty offences to which police personnel are party, directly by participating or by aiding, abetting, encouraging. The police seem to be going to ridiculous lengths to gain convictions, committing crimes worse than the persons they apprehended."

Vancouver lawyer Greg DelBigio, who spoke before the Commons Justice Committee, stated, "It is highly questionable whether it is consistent with the rule of law for police to break the law in order to enforce it. Police agents are typically themselves criminals and cannot be trusted or relied upon to abide by the law or follow a police officer's directions."

After four years of investigation, the study concluded in 1981, exonerating the security service and stating it was "ignorant of its own misdeeds." The report recommended that the powers of the RCMP be broadened rather than curtailed. It also led to the creation of a separate force whose sole mandate was to provide security within Canada. Hence, on July 16, 1984, the Canadian Security Intelligence Service, more commonly known as CSIS, came into being. Along with this new agency, a watchdog in the form of an Inspector General was established to oversee the agency's behavior; the latter would answer directly to the Deputy Solicitor General.

According to the Civil Liberties Association, Pierre Trudeau, the prime minister of Canada publicly stated, "The RCMP would not abuse its powers in the same manner as the FBI and CIA," and as for the activities of the security service, its powers should be broadened, rather than its criminal activities curtailed. Sidney Simons could only shake his head in disbelief.

In Simons' mind, the McDonald Commission fell far short of its intended goal but he never gave up his quest for a new system of justice. On three occasions, he has stood before all nine members of the Supreme Court of Canada to test the principle of police entrapment or abuse of process. On his third attempt, the magistrates voted nine to zero in favor of his argument, and this led to sweeping changes that would protect those like Williams, Elliott and Ridge.

E752 enjoying his retirement
Credit: E752

Map showing location of Hudson Is.
Credit: Web stock image

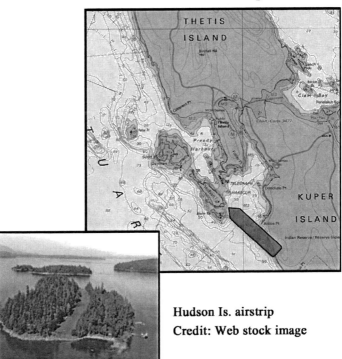

Hudson Is. airstrip
Credit: Web stock image

CHAPTER 22:

END OF THE LINE

*It was all working pretty well until the cops stumbled onto that
particular call to Ingrid.*

—Dale Elliott

On February 2, 1979, Dale Stuart Elliott ran out of places to hide. The
RCMP knew that sooner or later they would get their man. During the
eighteen months that he was on the lam, the Mounties had maintained
a watchful eye on his home and that of his parents. Elliott had a wife
with kids, and few men can vanish off the face of the earth without
maintaining some form of contact. In Elliott's case, they believed that
"sex was a staple of his life. Sooner or later he will have to reach out and
touch somebody."

As with the initial investigation, informants were everywhere and in
general terms, the media suggested they had again proved themselves
to be the meat of law enforcement. Moving about within their world of
closet espionage, the media incorrectly reported that one of the cop's
moles had encountered Elliott by chance at the Lynnwood Marina in
Lions Cove, North Vancouver. The cops figured Elliott would sooner or

later attempt to reach someone from his past so the RCMP tapped his home phone in addition to several other parties he associated with, but none of those aided their cause.

Then they got lucky.

While hiding off the grid, Elliott kept a lab running. In fact, within his first week on the run he had one in full production beneath the floorboards of the boat he was living on. He jerry-rigged a generator to the boat motor and picked up a rubber pump in Vancouver that put out 80 psi to work as an evaporator. Then he machined up a belt drive to connect the pump to the motor and this would take the mix through to the crystalline stage. In all, he was cooking about eight pounds of MDA at one time so he had no choice but to contact his buyers on a regular basis. When Dale needed to link up with Ingrid, he would tie up to a government wharf. There was always a pay phone close by. Whoever was with him at the time would jump off and call Ingrid with encrypted instructions as to which phone they would call her on next. Dale and Ingrid had all the numbers for pay phones in Duncan coded with names such as Jimmy or Joe. Every now and again absence would leave Dale with no choice but to fly her up to the Sunshine Coast for a conjugal visit.

In his words, "Ingrid was without a doubt my most trusted conduit. Just to mix things up and keep the cops off balance, I would have some of the buyers wait for me at a given wharf while others would grab a boat and come out to wherever I was cruising at that point in time. I never stayed in one place for more than a day but kept on the move to avoid contact with curiosity seekers."

At the same time the Mounties were winding down their ground search for Elliott, they were also conducting surveillance on an unrelated case in the Duncan area. Four pay phones, which they knew were used by their target, had been tapped, and while Chester Kary was reviewing the tapes one night, he heard a voice he thought he knew. He played it again.

"Sure enough," he said, "one voice was Ingrid Elliott's and the other was Dale's. By total happenstance I had stumbled onto Dale Elliott directing Ingrid to meet him at the Lynnwood Marina in North Vancouver.

Kary pulled a few of his crew together and followed her.

Although he was in possession of a .44 magnum and a .38 special, Elliott gave up without a struggle. Contrary to the media's report that he was tired of hiding, he says, "That's another bunch of crap. I was comfortable and making out real well. They just got me and the game was over. There would have been no value in grandstanding since I saw no benefit in going out in a blaze of glory."

Elliott had grown a moustache and goatee that had changed his appearance to such an extent that on one occasion his son Jerry didn't recognize him. For the benefit of those he came in contact with while on the run, Elliott had assumed the alias Charles Harmon, borrowed from a resident of Beaver Cove. He held a doctored passport with his new identity and a list of countries, which Don Bohun had given to him, that had no extradition treaty with Canada. The cops stated, there was every indication he was ready and able to make a one-way trip to friendlier soil.

At that point, Elliott offered the police a deal. In exchange for dropping a charge against him for carrying a restricted weapon and promising not to implicate his son's girlfriend, who was helping him on board to cook the MDA, he promised he would take them to his lab and plead guilty to a single charge of trafficking in MDA. Exhausted from the ongoing charade, the Crown prosecutor jumped at the offer.

Elliott was booked and detained in the cells of the North Vancouver RCMP detachment. The following morning, the officers on duty could hardly believe their eyes. Although they will never admit that their body search of Elliott was incomplete when they admitted him or, for that matter, that they did not keep an adequate watch on his cell during the night; by morning Elliott had removed his moustache and goatee. The media reported that Elliott had physically pulled out every hair by painful hair, but then again that was proven to be typical fake news. "Fact is," says Elliott, "I had an industrial razor blade in the watch pocket of my pants and the cops neglected to notice it when they locked me up. I just gave myself a shave during the night and then tossed the blade to the guy in the cell across from me when I was finished."

Before too many days had passed, Elliott kept his promise and led the Mounties to the isolated cabin on the shores of Salmon Inlet, north of Vancouver. This is where he had stored all the supplies he needed to continue with his production of MDA. It was clear as they entered the cabin that Elliott was provisioned sufficiently to keep the market satisfied for many months to come. A significant amount of lab equipment remained packed away in two large crates. The cops' only method of controlling the sale of Isosafrole had failed them bitterly, for Elliott had enough to produce an additional twenty pounds of pure MDA with a street value of roughly $3 million. With the profits going straight into Elliott's pocket, it would have been only a matter of days until he slipped through their nets one last time. As for the actual lab he had hidden beneath the floor boards of his boat, Elliott didn't feel inclined to share that piece of the puzzle with the cops per chance he might have some need for it in the future.

On April Fool's Day 1980, the last leg of the judicial marathon played itself out. Having won both earlier appeals before the BC Supreme Court and subsequently the Supreme Court of Canada following his 1973 conviction, Elliott appeared unconcerned about the outcome as he sat impassively in Victoria's county courthouse. A man of his word, he stood before Judge Peter Millward and pleaded guilty to the tabled 1973 charge of possessing MDA for the purposes of trafficking. He also entered a guilty plea to one count of trafficking in MDA arising out of the 1977 investigation. At long last the police realized the satisfaction that had evaded them over the preceding decade. Regina vs. Elliot had come to a close.

Dale Elliott, the man with strong ties to the notorious biker gangs of North America, had given them no fight from the day of his confinement. All the pent-up fear of what hell might rain down on their heads quickly faded into the court records as hearsay.

Elliott drew a four-year term for the 1973 conviction and a concurrent sentence for the 1977 conviction of trafficking. On April 1, 1980, he was led through the front gates of B.C.'s maximum-security prison in New Westminster. In time, he was moved to William Head, south of Victoria, so that he could be closer to his family, but he ended up getting sucked into a deal with a staff member that went sour. As a result, he lost his good-boy status and was shipped to the medium security facility of Matsqui where he worked as an electrician within the prison walls. In June 1981, a prison riot saw many inmates settling up a score with other prisoners as well as guards. At the close of the day, the prison was torched leaving it unfit for habitation. Elliott had stayed out of the fray so once the cops had regained control, Elliott and the others who were considered non-threatening were relegated to tents, where they stayed until space could be found for them in other institutions. Eventually Elliott was transferred to Elbow Lake, where he quietly finished his term.

The Crown immediately appealed the judge's decision, feeling Elliott's term was too lenient. That appeal failed, and Elliott served out his full term, by his own choice without parole, to avoid the hassle of having to report to a probation officer on a regular basis once the ordeal was over. Elliott and his wife separated shortly after that, with the family growing up and making their own statement on society. Long gone were the days when their hell-raising father shone the light on a path for them to walk. Dale Elliott's parents never served any time. In the eyes of the court, their entanglement in the case was merely a matter of being in the wrong place at the wrong time.

Like so many of his peers, Dale Elliott is confident that Arthur Williams died in the crash. "I don't know exactly what happened, but I do know Art was asked by E752, 'How would you bugger up a plane so it would crash and nobody could tell that it was tampered with?' to which Art replied, 'You would just put a piece of chewing gum over the intake tube located on the side of the cabin so it can't provide air to your gauges.' A few people including E752 knew that Art's plane was parked on the tarmac at Vancouver's south terminal that day."

As strange as all these events were, an incident eighteen months following Williams' disappearance cast an even longer shadow of doubt across the crash theory.

Dale Elliott (right) in William Head Pen
Credit: Dale Elliott

Dale Elliott (facing) in Elbow Lake Pen
Credit: Dale Elliott

CHAPTER 23:

NO FORWARDING ADDRESS

Wizard's wife vanishes and leaves behind a fortune.

—headline from the Victoria Times Colonist

During the endless hearings that involved her estranged husband, Margaret could always be found quietly sitting in the back row of the courtroom, offering to him what she believed to be her greatest asset, her endless support. With all the pain and humiliation Arthur had given her through his relationship with Shirley, she never once repaid his indiscretion with malice. If Margaret knew what profession her husband had been involved in, she never spoke a word about it. She repaid his many years caring for her materialistic needs with her undying loyalty.

In the weeks that followed the disappearance of her husband, Margaret busied herself around their Ladysmith farm. Somewhat frail from all the strife that had entered her life, Margaret puttered about in her garden, worked on her embroidery or her photography and continued to add to her nostalgic collection of bottles as the opportunity arose. She was never short of visitors during that time and most showed a degree of empathy for her inner turmoil by respecting her privacy enough not to pry into matters that didn't concern them.

Viv and Joy Marie, Margaret's neighbors, who lived directly across the highway, saw Margaret as a lovely host. "Viv and I were often invited over for tea, biscuits, and light conversation." Within a matter of days of the Marie's moving into the area, Margaret was at their door with some baked goods and a warm welcome into the neighborhood. Although Arthur was not as visible about the home, there was never any conversation that would lead Viv and Joy to believe her relationship with him was anything less than cordial. They say, "The fact that he lived with his girlfriend just a few feet away from where we enjoyed her company never came to our attention. Margaret just carried on as though everything was the way it should be. On occasions Arthur would wander in and pick up the conversation as though he had been there all along. He would interact with Margaret in a caring way, much like we would expect of any happily married couple. His interaction with us was always pleasant as was that of his wife. Over the years, they proved themselves to be splendid neighbors."

As the months wore on, Margaret's behavior took on a strange reflection of her late husband. Terry Ferguson shared that she packed away all her own clothes and began wearing Art's clothing. "She seemed to want to be Art and take over where he left off. Even the manner of her walking changed, and as she walked by, you would think it was Art with his long stride and heavy step."

In no time at all, problems of a different nature crept into her life. Parasitic people lusting for souvenirs of the community's notoriety wandered onto her property taking anything their hearts desired. Some of those who benefited from her husband's illicit activities came by and threatened her on issues she knew nothing about.

With the coroner's inquest complete, it took till April 8, 1978 for the declaration of death to make its way into Margaret's hands and another four months before she was awarded the issuance of probate from the Supreme Court of British Columbia. Regretfully, she never saw the benefit of either.

On March 6, 1979, just thirty-two days after Dale Elliott's arrest, Shirley Ferguson phoned Art's sister Ruth Dashwood to mention that Margaret's car had not moved off her property during the previous twenty-four hours, yet her home had remained unlit throughout the evening. Shirley wanted to know if she had stayed with the Dashwoods for the night. Ruth responded that she had not, and she too was sufficiently concerned that she made her way over to Margaret's home to confirm her absence.

Ruth Dashwood had last seen Margaret on March 1st. They had spent an hour or so together at Margaret's home, and according to Ruth, "She was her usual cheerful self, giving no indication of trouble, nor mentioning any plans for going away. She did however appear a bit edgy because her husband's estate still had not been settled."

There was no indication that it was a planned departure; only her cape and purse were missing. Her home was left as though she had just gone out for some needed groceries. The twist to that theory was that her car sat in the driveway and there was ample food in the house. All her clothes and personal effects were as they normally lay. None of her treasured keepsakes were missing, and her hair dryer was still plugged in and draped across the back of her sofa. Nothing was in disarray.

It was a month before the police opened a file on behalf of Margaret's disappearance. At that point, the matter was handed over to Nanaimo RCMP Corporal Maurice Fitzgerald, and while the case had grown cold, he refused to pass comment other than to say, "Although a motive has never been established, the release of any information would impair a homicide investigation." Fitzgerald mentioned that he did find a curious note on her kitchen table, but he wouldn't disclose its contents other than to say Margaret had been summarizing events that she wanted to remember at some date in the future. No one seemed willing to speculate toward the reason for her note.

Margaret's sister Rose Stelly, then living in Hinton, Alberta, mentioned that she had received a strange call from her sister four days before she was reported missing. Her sister, who had been caring for their father for sometime, was taken aback because Margaret knew their father had a practice of going to bed early and would be unable to come to the phone at such an hour. Nonetheless, the sisters talked for quite some time, yet spoke of nothing out of the ordinary. "Margaret was in a nostalgic mood and closed off by asking me to take good care of dad." Rose not only found it unusual, but the very nature of the call left her feeling peculiar.

Fitzgerald commented "It was as though Margaret was saying goodbye. If she was, it is unlikely she would have been kidnapped or murdered. How could she have known before the event?" Two possibilities remain to Fitzgerald's way of thinking: either Margaret left the area of her own free will, which supports the speculation that she may have joined her husband, or she committed suicide. Those who knew her feel strongly that Margaret would never have considered the latter of the two options.

As for those members of the public who thrive on the carnage of mankind, they have aligned themselves with a few of the immediate family who hold a strong conviction that she was murdered. They theorize that those on the fringe of her husband's production and distribution had illusions of carrying on in Williams' footsteps but could not do so without a bankroll to get started. It was common knowledge that Margaret kept large sums of money lying about her home, so if one were looking for a motive, it existed.

Art and Shirley's phone records for the latter part of 1977 indicate that they placed a few calls to a fellow within the 101 Knights who was well known for his ability "to lose things in a desert," so to speak. It is reported that Margaret employed this same fellow after her husband's disappearance to log the timber off their South Wellington property. The agreement, according to Shirley, was that Margaret would pay the guy when she received reimbursement from the sawmill, but "she ended up screwing him out of what she owed."

According to another fellow who was close to the couple, within a few days of Margaret's disappearance, this same fellow had boasted that he had knocked off some old lady, no name was mentioned. Yet another notorious character from the Ladysmith area professed to know who did her in. "Those responsible were former members of the 101 Knights and are very much alive today." It is no coincidence that, although none of these individuals have been in contact with each other for the past three decades, they all pointed to the same trigger person. Each felt justice was due, but not on their watch.

Shirley Ferguson suggested, "Margaret was in the process of gathering evidence against the RCMP's informant in the disappearance of her late husband when she vanished." Sid Simons, however, has gone on record as stating, "There was no substantiated evidence to back up suspicions E752 was connected with either of the Williams' disappearances. I can see people may have their suspicions, but until we find the main body of Art's aircraft, we'll never know exactly what happened."

In the months, preceding Art's disappearance, he had entrusted $90,000 to his friend Guy Antilla with instructions to share it equally between Margaret and Shirley in the event something should happen to him. Guy left the area shortly after for northern B.C., and in turn entrusted the money to Margaret for safekeeping on the understanding that her husband's wish would be carried out to the letter. Not wanting to part with Shirley's portion too quickly, Margaret stuffed it into a metal munitions case and hung it down a well at the back of her home. Shirley stated she knew where it was and kept an eye on it, "But I became suspicious of foul play when the canister vanished from its hiding spot two days prior to Margaret's disappearance."

Terry Ferguson, had returned from his weekly Boy's Club on the evening of Margaret's disappearance and made his routine visit to her cabin, where he would play the pump organ, which Arthur had built for her out of homemade parts, and devour hot chocolate and cookies. "I was certain someone was in there, but when I knocked on her door, no one answered. That had never happened to me before and, stranger than fiction, I recall seeing the silhouette of a hand in her living room window. Strange too was the fact that the dark-colored pickup driven by a fellow well-known to my family, and who had been a frequent late-night visitor of Margaret's, was parked just off to the side of our shared driveway."

Terry's brother Daniel feels that Terry may have witnessed a murder but has blanked it out of his memory.

Shirley recalls, "After Margaret went missing, I started getting all kinds of threatening telephone calls. Sometimes it was just heavy breathing, sometimes the words, 'Do you know where your kids are?' I started nailing the windows shut inside my home, and once when I came back from being out, all the nails were removed. It just got to a point where I couldn't take it any longer so I abandoned the property and moved back into Chemainus.

Shirley recalls; "In the months preceding Margaret's disappearance, Dave Ridge had dug a well on his property, just off the corner of his workshop. The thing was so deep he needed an extension ladder to get in and out. While that in itself is not unusual, within a day of Margaret's disappearance he had filled it in, saying it was no good. The fact that the Ridge boys despised Margaret was no secret. Margaret would really get their goat bossing them around, and they were both crazy enough to knock her off." When this view was shared with the fellow whose truck sat parked in Margaret's driveway that night, who also knew the Ridge boys well, and who preached that for one's health some things were best not repeated, he replied, "It wouldn't surprise me if there are a set of bones in that well. Fact is, there may be as many as three sets."

It has often been said by those wishing to stay anonymous, "The rural areas of the West Coast are as great a place to hide a body, as they are to hide those who are alive and well. It has absorbed its fair share of the wanted and unwanted, and unless there is a concerted effort by authorities to dislodge them, they can remain all but invisible for a lifetime."

Bev Nicholls [Ridge] recalls, "The night before Margaret disappeared, Ray gave me instructions to go over to her house because she had expressed an interest in buying his golf clubs. He gave me specific instructions as to when to arrive and when to leave and how to talk to Flipper [their dog] and the geese to get on and off the property. He didn't want me early and he didn't want me late. When I arrived, Margaret asked me if I wanted a cup of tea, but she was visibly nervous about something. The only other memory I have is that when Margaret was gone, Ray spent a considerable amount of time over there, digging her property up with Art's excavator, looking for money that she and Art had hidden. Ray never told me he had been involved in her disappearance, but he made it quite clear that he had been a bystander to at least three murders."

Once Fitzgerald got up and running with his investigation, he consumed two and a half years and hundreds of hours talking with family members and friends who may have known Margaret's whereabouts or may have spoken with her in the preceding days. Just on the chance she left the country under an alias, he made a trip to Ottawa where he spent an uneventful week going through thousands of passport photos. He circulated her description across Canada and the United States and conducted an intensive search throughout the local area, uncovering just one small fragment of information that cast doubt on the theory that she had joined Arthur.

In all the years, she and Arthur were together, Margaret seldom travelled, yet in the months preceding her disappearance she drove to California with her friend Ruth Loomis for what had previously been reported as a holiday. According to Ruth however, it was anything but a holiday. Margaret had heard that Williams had given Ruth's ex-husband, Gordon who had moved to California, a substantial amount of money roughly three months prior to his disappearance, and she felt she was entitled to it. Ruth said, Williams had given her husband strict instructions to hold the money, stating that he would return in a couple of months to collect it.

"It was hardly a relaxing trip. She cried for the whole ten days there and back. She just kept reliving the loss of Art over and over again." Once in Desert Hot Springs, Margaret arranged to meet Gordon Loomis in a small café to ask him about the $50,000 that Art had entrusted to him. Ruth plunked herself down in an adjacent booth so she could hear Margaret's conversation. "When Gordon came in, he sat with his back to me and had no idea I was there, and I could hear him clearly deny ever having received the money from Art."

After Art Williams disappeared, Lou Brown went south to work for Gordon Loomis. Gordon told Lou the cops had paid him a visit and laid out four passports on his kitchen table. One had a photo that was the spitting image of Art, but the date of issuance was after Art had disappeared. Constable Fitzgerald confirmed that he had interviewed Gordon following Margaret's disappearance but was not willing to offer further insight.

Daniel Ferguson offered the following information, "Two months prior to Art's disappearance, mom came across what I recall as being a birth certificate or passport in the name of Howard. Art saw her with it and took it away from her, saying it was not for her to see."

Coincidentally, but then again maybe not, following that fateful day in November 1977, Williams' lawyer Sid Simons had presented his statement to the McDonald Commission on Art's behalf. The clerk who received the statement was John F. Howard. That may not seem worthy of a second thought, but Williams never did anything without a hidden motive or purpose, even if it was just to stick a thorn into the ribs of yet another bureaucrat. Williams may have felt like encumbering Howard's good name in the same manner as he did with Inkster.

In the days that followed Margaret's disappearance, the media had a heyday with one sensational headline after another. On Saturday, August 1, 1981, the Victoria Colonist ran the headline "Wizard's wife vanishes and leaves behind a fortune." This kind of journalism only added to the trauma that Williams' sisters, Gladys and Ruth, and their respective families had to endure. Allen Dashwood speaks out, "The era when Arthur was dealing with the law and to some point beyond Margaret's disappearance, they were disturbing times for my family, and to be very honest, it has taken a long time for those wounds to heal. Arthur was a fascinating individual for me in my youth. He was full of adventure, creative in many things and always doing something around his home whether it was digging a hole or clearing his land. There was never a dull moment, but never did he give us cause to question his moral integrity."

After Margaret disappeared, all sorts of strange people showed up at the Dashwood home looking for information. The media were constant intrusions into their lives. Every cop on the face of the earth seemed to make repetitive enquiries about their mandate. Allen says, "People, whom we didn't know personally but knew were associated with Arthur, showed up for whatever reason my parents chose not to say. It was all scary and very unnerving for us. We didn't know where any of these visits would lead, nor if they would ever end."

On July 6, an anonymous call to the RCMP suggested that they would find a large sum of money buried near the cabin Margaret had called home. The lead was followed and $57,300, wrapped in bundles and stuffed in a plastic ice-cream container, was recovered from her woodpile. If Margaret was intending to flee the country, Fitzgerald wanted someone to clarify why she would leave such a large sum of money behind. Was she in such a hurry when she left that she forgot to retrieve it? Was the $57,300 such a minuscule amount in comparison to what was tucked away in foreign accounts that it was more trouble than it was worth to recover and transport? How much money did Williams' courier to Belize in April 1977? Ralph Harris offered, "The money that was left with Gordon Loomis was destined for the Grand Cayman Islands. After running into conflict with the Cubans, Art left it with Gordon rather than bring it back into Canada." So many questions remain with so few answers.

As the police systematically moved through Margaret's home, looking for clues to her disappearance, they came across a statement from a bank in Europe that, per the police, held a small amount of money on deposit. Bev Nicholls adds, "Prior to Art's disappearance, there were conversations with Ray about foreign bank accounts in the Cayman Islands, Cuba and the Dominican Republic. I was never a participant in these conversations but rather an observer; therefore, I don't know anything more than that."

Drawn by the prospect of finding buried treasure, fortune seekers from throughout the region turned up in droves at the property. You would have thought it was Ground Zero or Dieppe on the day the Allies landed. There were bunker-sized holes dug all over the place, and everything that could move was turned over. Allen Dashwood was disgusted. "They pilfered everything except the kitchen sink. They even stole the tractor and backhoe. There were so many personal items taken as trophies, that we as a family, found little of value when we went over to clean the place up. Margaret's photos, Art's library, all mementos of their lives together were gone."

Faster than the unanswered questions could be pushed aside, new ones popped up. Not long after Margaret's disappearance, both the large lab and Margaret's cabin were destroyed by fire. Ladysmith fire Chief Bill Grouhel said investigators suspected arson because "the house was burning in separate, unrelated places – the northwest and east ends of the building. There is every indication that a petroleum product was used because of the extremely black smoke."

Who set the fires and why?

The police had absolutely no clue and pondered whether it was anything more than a case of willful damage. Stanley Cross repeats the promise Williams made before he disappeared. "He stated that he would never leave anything for the government to benefit from if something was to happen to him. He would burn the place to the ground." Stanley wasn't surprised when it happened and feels it confirms that Williams is still alive. "There will come a time when Art will make his presence known just long enough to rub the authorities' nose in his escape."

Williams' neighbor, Joy Marie, added, "On numerous occasions while Art was around, a small plane would fly low overhead. This we came to understand was the method he used to summon Margaret or one of his inner circle to drive to the Cassidy Airport and pick him up after a trip abroad. Late at night, not long after Margaret's disappearance, a single-engine plane flew low over our home just like it had through the preceding years. Viv and I didn't think too much about it until roughly 2 a.m., when we were woken by sirens moving towards us from all directions. When we got up to see what all the commotion was about, the Williams cabin was a hellish inferno."

With theories coming from every corner, Happy Laffin recalls, "After Art disappeared, I kept an eye on Margaret per chance she needed something. It didn't matter whether it was a plugged toilet or a load of firewood, I was there to help. Everybody knew I kept an eye on her, and then, after she disappeared, I maintained an interest in the well-being of their property per chance she came back. One day Ray Ridge confronted me at a construction site and told me Margaret's place and the lab were going up the next night. Sure as shooting, the place was nothing but a pile of ash by morning. Ken Sutherland of the RCMP still finds it suspicious that the burn would take place just as people started to dig into Williams' past. Art had told those he associated with that he was keeping a diary of names and events should any one of them decide to stab him in the back. It appears someone had reason to ensure that little book never fell into the wrong hands. According to Ray Ridge, individuals had rummaged through every corner of the home and lab with no success and resolved the only way to insure the diary was gone was to burn the place and all its contents to the ground.

To this day, if anyone knows of Margaret's whereabouts, they are not talking. No airline company, point of customs entry or any other such resource has a record of her movements. She, like Art, has simply vanished.

Art Williams' mycology & MDA lab following fire
Credit: Daryl Ashby

CHAPTER 24:

THE LAST WORD

I often wished that he had channeled his intelligence into something more useful. I'm rather sad to think he could have done so much.

—Gladys Little

Four decades have now passed since Art Williams vanished. Many of those who were part of his inner circle have died, while those who pursued him are enjoying what they consider to be a well-deserved retirement.

Shirley Ferguson still resides in the area and continues to open her door to young adults who have not fared well in mainstream society. Terry Ferguson became an accomplished automotive mechanic, but an injury left him the recipient of a disability pension. Daniel Ferguson took up drywalling and now manages a large drywall firm in Alberta.

Dale Elliott passed away in Sept. 2016. His celebration of life was a fitting gathering representing a diverse cross section of his life. His ex-wife, Ingrid, passed away some twenty years prior from asthma-related problems. Their children have scattered to the four corners of the Pacific Northwest. His son Steve proudly carries the colors that his father once considered vogue. According to Dale, Jerry has lost himself in a fictional world, adopting the identity of Talisman. Michael Elliott, who was said to have been the most levelheaded member of the family, lost his life a decade or so back after finding shelter for the night beneath his parked transport truck. He was curled up in his sleeping bag when some mindless individual disengaged the parking brake. The last brother Raymond walks a fairly straight and narrow path as a long-haul driver, while Dale's daughter Mona now has a family of her own.

Ray Ridge passed away March 5, 2006. Having spent a good number of years gaining a quick high from heroin and marking his years behind bars with prison tattoos, he succumbed to the ill effects of dirty needles like so many of his associates. His brother David took his own life in 2004 with the aid of a handgun. Some suggest it wasn't suicide but, rather a settling of old debts. Whatever the cause, it is well-known he was fighting depression at the time over the loss of a relationship.

Don Lovo was considered a success story in his own right. Yet at a time when he should have been absorbed in fond memories, he settled for a self-inflicted exit in May 2006 at the muzzle end of one of his many handguns.

It is rumored Myron Zarry died after falling into a lumber mill's head saw where he worked on the Lower Mainland, but that cannot be confirmed.

Lou Brown followed a girlfriend to New Zealand, where he took up commercial fishing before returning to the interior of British Columbia. His eldest son found himself drawn into the arena of fast money and sadly took his life in March 2009 after an international drug sting scooped him up south of the border.

Ruth Loomis defined herself as an activist and has published a few short stories that are worth the read. Gordon Loomis died several years back, while their daughter Kristine is happily married and has been living in the California desert fighting at a political level for the rights of those who are physically challenged.

Dave Staples, Bob Hawkes, Jerry Moloci, Chester Kary and Pat Convey are all retired from the RCMP. On the heels of Elliott's conviction, Kary and two of his buddies found their lives thwarted by an officer who is said to have leaned on a desk for the better part of his career and who couldn't hold his own in the real world if he had to. This fellow made $40,000 a year more than the boys on the ground and had spun the disappearance of Arthur and Margaret into an internal investigation. In this fellow's mind, there was an overwhelming motive to suggest that Kary, E752 and Hawkes had conspired to kill both Art and Margaret. As time passed, word came down from Gordon McDougall, who sat as the commanding officer of the Victoria Division, to 'forget it and never bring it up again.'"

While it is too late to play a part in the internal investigation, E752 goes on record as saying, "The week prior to Art crashing, I took a wax imprint of his planes' key at the request of someone involved in the investigation. You can't kill a guy and call it an accident. On the day he crashed, I was in Quebec, yet I could have stopped the whole thing in its tracks but I didn't. Now I have to take that to my grave." When he was asked, who directed him to make an imprint of the key, he refused to comment.

Whatever the case, the informant has found himself in and out of trouble since the day Kary gave him a new identity. He spent a few anxious months in a Mexican jail after stuffing his motor home and a catamaran sailboat with Mexican grass. Not enjoying the Mexican hospitality, he disguised himself as an old man and executed a daring escape as the weekly visitors made their exit. From there he made straight for the US border in route to familiar soil in Canada. That story was ghost written by Michael Dorgan and entitled "Escape from Guadalajara." Rumors suggest he is now state side, working off his marker with the DEA, while others hint that he has gone east to reconnect with his French-Canadian roots.

Williams' easy-going lawyer Don Bohun retired in 2003 to a tropical beach in Central America where, as he puts it, "You're either wanted or unwanted. Most everyone here is either running from drug-related charges or retired from the trade."

The informant Stanley Cross is fighting hepatitis C brought on by years of needle abuse and remains hunkered down under witness protection.

As for the hundreds of other characters entwined in the story of Arthur James Williams, the list goes on, but so do the unanswered questions. Some of the residents of Ladysmith continue to place credence on the fake death scenario. They believe Arthur Williams is one man smart enough to cheat death. "Alive? Oh, sure he's alive," says John MacNaughton, a close friend of Williams and the former publisher of the Ladysmith-Chemainus Chronicle. "No question about it. He's too clever and plans too well. He was a tremendously intelligent man, one of the most intelligent I ever met. He was a character with some unusual ideas. In the early days, Art had a friend in Powell River who owed him money, so he decided to go and collect it. But Art didn't have the money to get to Powell River, so he tried to borrow $10 from the bank. The bank manager turned him down. Not to be stopped, Williams cashed a 'rubber' cheque for $10 on Friday, went to Powell River and collected his money, and put $10 in the bank account on Monday to cover the overdraft. He is a survivor!"

There is as much speculation floating around about Williams living somewhere in the tropics as there is for the American D.B. Cooper, who hijacked a Boeing 727 on November 24, 1971, and parachuted out of the plane with $200,000 in ransom money, never to be seen again.

The disappearance of Margaret gave the Mounties new vigor to consider more seriously the possibility that Williams was living comfortably in some remote tropical paradise. Rumors and speculation about his possible whereabouts have continued to surface, with reported sightings in Central America and the Caribbean. Several people in the Ladysmith area suggested that they have seen him since his disappearance or received mail from him.

Ruth Dashwood states, "I approached these people who claim they have seen him and asked them why they haven't reported it to the police. They won't say and I can get no satisfaction from them." One of those people is Dirk Yzenbrandt. Dirk knew Art from the Victoria (Airport) Flying Club and states he saw Williams in 1983 and he still recalls the moment quite clearly. "I was a stockbroker with the Victoria branch of Merrill Lynch in the 800-block Douglas Street in 1983. I was on my lunch hour and walking north on Douglas, and I recognized Art walking towards me. I was within six feet of him and I went to acknowledge him, but as soon as he made eye contact he made an abrupt right turn into a little magazine store. I was somewhat stunned at first by seeing him and then by how he reacted, so I kept walking. After a few paces I figured this was stupid, so I turned around, determined to confront him. Within a matter of seconds, he came out of the store and made a beeline in the opposite direction. I reported my sighting to the cops, but to the best of my knowledge they did nothing."

Constable Maurice Fitzgerald commented that he was aware of the rumors, but "none of the sightings have been substantiated." Having said that, he adds, "Consider that in 1977 Williams was living with a girlfriend, but he retained a very close friendship with his wife, Margaret. Consider the odds of two people in a small community disappearing. Consider the odds that those two were married."

Has the man who despised the Canadian tax-grabbing mentality found security in the warmer climates of a tropical country? Two years after his disappearance, did he return under the cover of darkness to ensure that Margaret would join him during his remaining years? What business did he and his lawyer involve themselves with while in Belize and the Caymans?

Williams' nephew Pat Little states, "I know there was an inquest after the crash and he was declared dead, but to this day I have never accepted that verdict. Now that his wife has vanished, I am even more skeptical. Arthur could easily have faked his death and later come back to collect Margaret to live somewhere in seclusion."

Art Williams' sister Gladys reflects, "I often wondered what could have steered Art into such deep waters. Certainly, it was not greed. Material things were not particularly important to him. He never lived like a person with great wealth. He never appeared to have a great deal. I often wished that he had channeled his intelligence into something more useful. I'm rather sad to think he could have done so much. He could have turned out so differently, but no one had been there to guide his restless and troubled youth following his mother's death so many years before.

"Art never spoke to us about the illegal stuff, but I do recall on one occasion when he came to visit us in Edmonton, that he spoke of how he would make his escape by faking an airplane accident. I don't put much faith in the theory that he staged a crash. That's really ludicrous. There are so many silly speculations. I don't think there's any doubt that the plane went down."

Gladys has stewed over every detail of the crash for so long that she is convinced her brother had instrument troubles and honestly thought he was flying at 1,000 feet. Besides, she says, "Parachuting out of a plane over water wouldn't have been Art's chosen method of disappearance. He didn't swim, so he didn't like the water. That would have been like committing suicide. He was an extremely intelligent man. If he was trying to escape, I think he would have found a better way than to risk his life.

"The only mystery in my mind is why he was flying that night at all. He didn't like flying at night. I'm really at a loss as to why he would fly that night if there was any question whatsoever. I always knew him to be very, very careful when it came to his own safety. I've wondered at times if somebody did something to his plane, but he always checked it thoroughly before he flew." She is confident, however that her brother would be amused by the speculation surrounding his life and death. "That would please him. If nothing else, he would be happy to know that he's got so many people baffled."

Ten different fiction writers could come up with ten plausible explanations for what happened, but all the evidence would leave doubt overshadowing each theory.

The men who worked so hard to see Arthur James Williams brought to justice enjoyed a bitter victory. What they uncovered came to be known as the largest MDA operation in the history of North America. Unlike other crime families, once Ridge and Elliott were removed from the scene and Williams was reported dead, there was no hierarchy left to carry on. The flow of MDA all but dried up following Elliott's incarceration; that is until late in 1978, when a source outside the Mounties' reach started the kettles boiling once again. The RCMP chemist has said that the MDA Williams produced had a specific signature in its chemical arrangement, different from that of Elliott's. This new product held a strong resemblance to both.

The Attorney General has refused to allocate any additional funds for further research. Other than the convictions of Elliott and Ridge, all they have for their efforts are a number of boxes full of photographs and miscellaneous pieces of evidence that one day may be used to unravel the puzzle.

Whatever the case, Arthur James Williams has never stood trial for the charges laid against him on August 16, 1977. According to Canadian law, he is still an innocent man. As journalist Lee King put it: "Brilliant and arrogant in life, he remains an enigma." What lingers in the past, and just maybe in the future, is a man referred to in drug circles as a genius and a wizard. Now, in presumed death, he has become a legend. The secrets hidden behind the dark eyes in his faded pictures have vanished as perfectly, completely and mysteriously as Arthur James Williams himself.

ACKNOWLEDGMENTS

This book is only made possible by the willingness of many people who shared their memories of the events that transpired within Arthur Williams' subculture. This openness came from both sides of the law and many points in between.

I particularly want to acknowledge the generosity of Judge Les Cashman, who graciously opened his judicial records to my scrutiny. A special word of gratitude goes to the secretarial Office of the Vancouver Appeals Court and the master's secretary of the Nanaimo Supreme Court for granting me access to files pertinent to Williams' 1974 trial.

The expert journalism of Derek Sidenius and Lee King of the *Victoria Times* and the *Victoria Colonist* turned out to be the starting point for my research, and several areas within this book reflect their work.

A special note of gratitude goes to Gladys Little, Arthur Williams' youngest sister, for sharing with me family photos and intimate details of their childhood, also to Allen Dashwood, son of Arthur Williams' sister Ruth, for his vivid memory of Art during his own impressionable years.

Shirley Ferguson, Art's common-law wife at the time of the story's climax, has been guarded about her memories as I sense she has fear of saying too much. As for her sons, Terry and Daniel, they were ready and willing to gain a better understanding of their past and both offered a unique twist from a child's perspective.

Ruth (Shorter) Loomis sat with me for a number of hours and shared personal letters that she had received from Art in the early 70s. Credit also goes to Dave Staples, George (Bob) Hawkes, Chester Kary, Pat Convey,

Brian Froats and Jerry Moloci, all now retired from the RCMP, for their clarification of so many details which up till now had not been recorded.

Appreciation goes to Bill and Janice Sampson, for showing me samples of the Williams' bow that they have in their collection. The same if not more so can be said of Al Wills, who by his deep-rooted love of archery maintains an archive of every bow manufactured and a library of literature marketing the Williams' bow, plus articles penned by Art Williams.

Victor (Happy) Laffin was an early associate of Williams and pointed me towards several details, which were privy to him alone.

I would like to show my appreciation to Ralph Harris, who was a close friend of Williams since the early 1950s. Bev Nicholls for her vivid memory of events surrounding Ray Ridge. Sid Simons, the man who defended the primary characters associated with this story, has been more than generous with his time. Don Bohun, the flamboyant lawyer who stood by Art Williams through the good and bad times maintains he has no knowledge of what went on behind closed doors.

To the late Dale Elliott, the man who earned his bones as Williams' right-hand man and his only true confident, held little to nothing back. To his mind, "It's about time the story was told." To him I owe the greatest respect and appreciation for without him so much of this story would never have been told.

I would be remiss if I didn't express my appreciation for my editors, Audrey McClellan and Melva McLean, for without them I would be nothing more than a man with a fist full of notes.

Last but definitely not least, there is the unconditional support of my wife, Wendy and daughters Cheryl and Barbara, during the lengthy process of writing, for their encouragement and input after reading the preliminary draft.

So many people have contributed towards this work, yet you can be assured I have surely missed some. For those who have slipped through the cracks, I sincerely apologize, for without you this book would not be possible.

BIBLIOGRAPHY

- Times Newspaper
- Colonist Newspaper
- The Vancouver Sun
- B.C. Provincial Archives
- Judge Cashman's personal case notes
- Vancouver Appeals Court Library
- Office of Supreme Court Trial Master's Secretary

Non-published:

- Interview with Jason Grist, air traffic controller Vancouver International Airport
- Interview with Mr. & Mrs. V. Marie of Ladysmith, 1978
- Interview with Bob Hawkes, retired RCMP
- Interview with Jerry Moloci, retired RCMP
- Interview with Victor (Happy) Laffin
- Interview with Al Wills, Canadian Archery
- Interview with Dale Elliott
- Interview with Bev Nicholls, wife to Ray Ridge
- Interview with Dave Staples, retired RCMP
- Interview with Pat Convey, retired RCMP
- Interview with Blaine Froats, retired RCMP
- Interview with Chester Kary, retired RCMP
- Interview with Dewy Babcock, associate of informant E752

- Interview with Shirley Ferguson, common-law wife of Art Williams
- Interview with Gladys Little, Art Williams' sister
- Interview with Daniel Ferguson, son of Shirley
- Interview with Terry Ferguson, son of Shirley
- Interview with Ralph Harris, associate of Ray Ridge & Art Williams
- Interview with Krisy Morrison, friend Ray Ridge
- Interview with Don Bohun, Art & Dale's lawyer

Published:

- Porter, Bruce. *Blow.* US: Harper Collins Publisher, Inc., 1993
- Underground Empire
- *The Canadian Archer,* published 1963 thru, publisher & editor John A. MacNaughton
- Murdock, Derrick. *Disappearances,* Pinnacle Books, New York, ISBN 0523 43198-8

ABOUT THE AUTHOR

 Daryl Ashby has developed a reputation for searching out subjects poorly analyzed or scarcely recorded, capturing unnoticed details that could possibly change public perception, as well as the implausible landscapes that our minds conveniently map.

As a local historian and journalist he takes great pride insuring his work is as accurate as physically possible cutting no corners when it comes to digging at the truth refusing to shelter those who warrant exposure for their past no matter what the risk.

If you enjoy this read, you will also enjoy his first person account "John Muir: West Coast Pioneer", published by Ronsdale Press. This book provides an engaging account of the first 30 years in the Colony of Vancouver Island, the foundation for what later became known as British Columbia, Canada. No other man singularly contributed as much to establish the settlement of the Pacific Northwest.

Daryl's presentation of John Muirs' life and his related activities in and around the colony has been suitably recognized as a runner up to the prestigious BC Book Prize award as well as the Victoria-Butler Book Prize.

CPSIA information can be obtained
at www.ICGtesting.com
Printed in the USA
LVOW10s1908060518
576236LV00003B/6/P

9 781773 703503